Anointing
the
Unsanctified

Anointing the Unsanctified

Dr. Mark Hanby

Destiny Image® Publishers, Inc.
P.O. Box 310
Shippensburg, PA 17257-0310

"Speaking to the Purposes of God for this Generation"

ISBN 1-56043-071-0

For Worldwide Distribution
Printed in the U.S.A.

Second Printing: 1998   Third Printing: 1999

This book and all other Destiny Image, Revival Press, and Treasure House books are available at Christian bookstores and distributors worldwide.

For a U.S. bookstore nearest you, call **1-800-722-6774**.
For more information on foreign distributors, call **717-532-3040**.
Or reach us on the Internet: **http://www.reapernet.com**

Contents

Chapter 1

Prayer and the Anointing

Wherefore the law was our schoolmaster to bring us unto Christ....

Galatians 3:24

Now all these things happened unto them for ensamples: and they are written for our admonition, upon whom the ends of the world are come.

I Corinthians 10:11

He made known His ways unto Moses, His acts unto the children of Israel.

Psalm 103:7

In order to obtain an understanding of Christ and of His mission and purpose for His Church, we must go to the old schoolmaster (the Old Testament and the Law.) In it is recorded everything that happened to Moses and Israel. Those events are examples for us. They are also "ensamples." Ensamples are acted-out stories of things that we can physically see. God would show Moses what to do and the children of Israel would act it out. So they "acted out" what is being done in the Church. They acted it out and we are to experience it.

1

The Law, however, is not the very image of the things of God. Rather, it is a shadow. "For the law having a shadow of good things to come...."[1] How do you create a shadow? You shine a light across some object. Here the light of the glory of God in the face of Jesus Christ shines back on the cross and casts a shadow. That shadow is the tabernacle, and the Old Testament Law.

Moses' tabernacle was a shadow of things to come. When Moses said, "Show me Your glory," the Lord took him up into the mountain and shone the light of Heaven across the heavenly sanctuary so the shadow that fell on the earth was the shadow of the real sanctuary in the heavens.[2] It is with that heavenly sanctuary that the church today is concerned.

Don't Touch Me

Let's begin with a seeming contradiction in Jesus after His resurrection. When He was risen and Mary was wandering around outside His tomb, she saw a man she presumed to be the gardener. She said to him, "Sir, tell me where you have laid Him." He turned around and said, "Mary." She said, "Rabboni." She recognized that it was Jesus. She reached out to touch Him, and He said, "Touch Me not for I have not yet ascended. I must ascend to your God and to My God. Don't touch Me."[3]

A little later Jesus appeared in a room with His disciples and said, "Thomas, come here. Touch Me. Put your finger in the print of the nail. Here, thrust your hand into My side. It is I."[4]

Why would He tell one person, after His resurrection, "Don't touch Me," and tell another, "Come, touch Me"? Something must have happened in the interim. Why not ask the old schoolmaster?

"Schoolmaster, why wasn't Mary supposed to touch Jesus?"

"Because He was the high priest of our profession. He freely offered Himself as a sacrifice."

What exactly does that mean? The Law says that no man was to be in the tabernacle when the high priest went to sprinkle the blood of the sacrifice on the mercy seat between the cherubim.[5] He had to be alone. So in this situation, the old schoolmaster teaches us that Jesus, being the high priest and the fulfillment of the shadow in the old, had not yet ascended into the heavenly sanctuary (the real tabernacle of which Moses' was only a shadow). Jesus had to ascend up and walk through the heavenly sanctuary, carrying His own blood, "the blood of sprinkling, that speaketh better things than [the blood] of Abel."[6] Jesus, the High Priest, then sprinkled His blood on the mercy seat in Heaven.

Wherefore He saith, When He ascended up on high, He led captivity captive, and gave gifts unto men.

Ephesians 4:8

It was at this point that He determined to give the fullness of God to the earth. "I will give this fullness to the apostleship, the high priestship, and the evangelist ministry. I will do it in a five-faceted ministry."[7] Then He led captivity captive, gave gifts to men, came back down and said, "You can touch Me now. It's finished."

Smiting the Rock

If everything that happened to Moses in the Law was a type and shadow of things to come in Christ, then why was Moses not allowed to enter the promised land? The answer: He had hit the rock twice. The first time the Lord said, "Smite the rock." Moses smote it and water came out of the rock.[8] The second time the Lord said, "Speak to the rock," but Moses struck the rock again. He was angry with the people and so smote the rock.[9]

The Lord said, "I appreciate all you've done for Me, buddy, but that's it. I can't use you anymore."

First Corinthians chapter 10 teaches that the Israelites were all baptized of Moses in the cloud and the sea and that all ate the manna and drank the water from that rock. The rock that followed them in the wilderness was Christ.

Christ was smitten only once. "But now once in the end of the world hath He appeared to put away sin by the sacrifice of Himself."[10] Thus Moses was untrue to the pattern. He hit the rock twice. Jesus should have been smitten only once and never crucified again. After that, we just speak to the rock and out of it comes water. (Water represents the Spirit.)

The Apothecary's Work

So what else is a type or shadow of things to come? In the tabernacle, besides the high priest, there was the apothecary, or the chemist priest. His sole responsibility was to make anointing oil and incense. His work also has a spiritual application for us today.

The apothecary used various compound substances to make the anointing oil.[11] Cassia is the tenderness inside the cambium of the tree, the hopes and dreams of the tree. The calamus is the scrapings from the root of the sweet sugar cane tree. Cinnamon is the grinding of the inner bark. Myrrh is the bleeding of the branch, its brokenness and hurt. The apothecary combined all these substances with oil, without allowing them to ferment and become bitter. Thus the anointing should not produce anger, nastiness, derision or questioning against God. The priest offered to God all these substances in oil, saying in type, "I give You my hurt, my joy, my hopes and my fears. I give You my good and my bad. In everything, I give You thanks. This is the will of God concerning me in Christ Jesus."[12] We create this ointment, aroma and oil from these things so we may anoint and pour them out upon our headship, upon the work of the Lord, and upon the ministry. That is the anointing.

Incense was the other substance created by the apothecary.[13] The high priest poured the incense out on hot coals of fire in the golden altar in front of the veil, sending up an aroma in the tabernacle of the Lord. When the Lord smelled it, He came out from His hiding place behind the veil and met the priest at the golden altar.

We need to ask the old schoolmaster what that means.

"Schoolmaster, what is that?"

"That's an altar."

"What is being put on the altar?"

"A compound substance of four different ingredients mixed all together with oil. It's poured on the altar on hot coals. Then it goes up to God and makes a sweet-smelling savor."

"Yes, but that's all physical. What does it mean spiritually?"

To answer this question, we need to address a different part of the old schoolmaster.

Men and brethren, let me freely speak unto you of the patriarch David, that he is both dead and buried, and his sepulchre is with us unto this day. Therefore being a prophet, and knowing that God had sworn with an oath

> **to him, that of the fruit of his loins, according to the**
> **flesh, He would raise up Christ to sit on his throne; he**
> **seeing this before spake of the resurrection of Christ,**
> **that His soul was not left in hell, neither His flesh did see**
> **corruption.**
>
> Acts 2:29-31

David, being a prophet and seeing all these things before-hand, will give us a spiritual answer to what the altar of incense typifies.

> **Lord, I cry unto Thee: make haste unto me; give ear**
> **unto my voice, when I cry unto Thee. Let my prayer be**
> **set forth before Thee as incense; and the lifting up of my**
> **hands as the evening sacrifice.**
>
> Psalm 141:1-2

Those were the actions done in the tabernacle. The incense had to be kept burning day and night. It was said, "See that the fire go not out on the altar of incense."[14] When it burned a little low, the priest of the Lord would come in and pour on more incense. This incense that continually spirals up is the aroma of prayer. "Let my prayer be set forth before Thee as incense."

In the New Testament, we find this passage:

> **Pray without ceasing. In every thing give thanks: for**
> **this is the will of God in Christ Jesus concerning you.**
>
> I Thessalonians 5:17-18

Why is it the will of God? Go ask the old schoolmaster.

"You cannot let the fire go out. Your whole attitude and spiritual mentality must be that of continually offering your subconscious and your mental attitude to God."

We must be God-ward in our living.

"This little altar and the incense being poured on it," the schoolmaster tells us, "is the type of the continual prayer of the saints, ascending up before God."

The Incense of Prayer

And when He had taken the book, the four beasts and four and twenty elders fell down before the Lamb, having every one of them harps, and golden vials full of odours, which are the prayers of saints.

Revelation 5:8

And when He had opened the seventh seal, there was silence in heaven about the space of half an hour. And I saw the seven angels which stood before God; and to them were given seven trumpets. And another angel came and stood at the altar, having a golden censer; and there was given unto him much incense, that he should offer it with the prayers of all saints upon the golden altar which was before the throne.

Revelation 8:1-3

Just as the tabernacle of Moses was merely the shadow cast on the earth when the glory shined across the real sanctuary, the altar of incense was just a shadow of the real altar in Heaven. The incense at this altar is all the prayers of the saints. The angels of the Lord are constantly taking the prayers of the saints of God to this altar.

Thou tellest my wanderings: put Thou my tears into Thy bottle: are they not in Thy book?

Psalm 56:8

Every time you shed a tear, an angel of the Lord catches it. When you pray for your lost son or daughter, every prayer and every tear is bottled up and poured out on the golden altar in Heaven. Your prayer is holy incense poured out by the angels of God.

And the angel took the censer, and filled it with fire of the altar, and cast it into the earth: and there were voices, and thunderings, and lightnings, and an earthquake.

Revelation 8:5

The angel took the things that were caught in the bottle, the prayers and tears of the saints, put them in the censer, and cast them back down to the earth. The prayers of saints go up, they are poured on the altar and then they are cast back on the earth. The answer of God shakes the earth. What is sealed in the earth is sealed in Heaven. What you bind in earth is bound in Heaven. What you loose on earth is loosed in Heaven.[15]

We must learn how this compound substance is created in the Law in order to know how, in the spiritual realm, to create a prayer with an aroma that can open the windows and doors of Heaven for us to enter His presence.

The Components of the Anointing Oil and Incense

And the Lord said unto Moses, Take unto thee sweet spices, stacte, and onycha, and galbanum; these sweet spices with pure frankincense: of each shall there be a like weight: and thou shalt make it a perfume, a confection after the art of the apothecary, tempered together, pure and holy: and thou shalt beat some of it very small, and put of it before the testimony in the tabernacle of the congregation, where I will meet with thee: it shall be unto you most holy.

Exodus 30:34-36

Both the anointing oil and the incense used the same four spices in this offering, the work and art of the apothecary.

Let's take a look at these spices by considering the original Hebrew meaning of these words from *Strong's Exhaustive Concordance of the Bible* (James Strong, *The Exhaustive Concordance of the Bible,* Peabody, MA: Hendrickson Publishers, n.d.). (These meanings also come from their prime root words and so may not be exact to *Strong's*.)

Stacte (#5198): It means, in short, an aromatic gum that drops continually, as in a process of distillation. It is something that is crushed and distilled.

Going beyond the physical aspect of these spices, I can tell you that one of these means "exaltation and joy." One means "the washing of purity." One means "upright," which goes back to the bleeding of the branch and to suffering. So prayer is taking your good times, your bad times, your happy things, and your sad things, and giving them all to Jesus. You do the same thing with incense that you do with the anointing oil because these spices mean the same things.

Onycha (#7827): It is the inside scraping of the mother of pearl from a seashell, but the original word means "that which is sought out of the depths."

Therefore, if we want to learn to pray, we must be willing to let something in our life be crushed so there is a constant dropping, a distillation, in our life—a continual dropping of spiritual fervor. We must be willing to go down deep into the ocean of God's purpose and take something from what we find in our life there.

Galbanum (#2464): It is "an odorous gum," but it goes back to #2459, which is the "fat." It is the richest or choicest part of thyme.

Thus, we do not give to God what is left over. We give Him the richest and fattest part our life.

Frankincense (#3828): It means "whiteness," but if you follow it back to the prime root, it is **laban,** which means "white." Number 3828, however, is **lebonah,** which means "whiteness" or what seems to be clear or pure. That word then goes back to #3885, the prime root. That's where it all started, before it had an evolution of meanings. This prime root means "to stop (usually over night)"; "to stay permanently"; to "abide (all night), continue...endure...lie all night"; to "tarry" through the night, to be intimate with. The word **frankincense** comes from a root that means to stay all night.

There was an idea in the original language of a purity in the bed of marriage. This root is interpreted to mean that you "tarry all night with the purity of one with a maiden." That brings glory to God. Proverbs calls it the mystery "of a man with a maid."[16] There is an intimacy like a pure relationship with God, spending the night with Him.

We Are Creators of Incense

Such a study of the anointing and of the holy anointing oil reveals that the glory of God is not what God puts on us, but something we offer Him. We are the glory producers. We are the creators of incense, like the apothecaries of the Law.

Thus, we need to pray in the correct way, according to the pattern. It requires an equal amount from each ingredient. When they are combined together and poured out on the hot coals of the altar, it creates an aroma that pleases God. Then He makes with us at-one-ment (atonement). The *atonement* means at-one-ment with God. We can be "at one" with God.

Let something come out of your spirit that is a continual distillation. Let whatever is in you come out constantly in prayerful drops. Plunge down to the depths of the ocean of your experience, take from it the treasures hardest to reach, and offer all of it together with a hin of oil.

Sometimes you must say it over again until you beat it small. You go over it again and again. When you are finished, pour that out over the coals of your fire.

We have never learned how to pray. We simply found one substance that God liked, threw it on the altar just any old way and thought that we had prayed. No, prayer is a compound substance; it is not a single thing. Prayer is not prayed. Prayer is made. We must have an equal amount of each substance, each ingredient, or God cannot receive it.

And on the sabbath we went out of the city by a river side, where prayer was wont to be made; and we sat down, and spake unto the women which resorted thither.

Acts 16:13

Paul went down to the river where the women were, where prayer was usually made. They made prayer there by the river. They had learned the art of spiritual sacrifice at the golden altar. Can we do as well?

End Notes

1. Hebrews 10:1.
2. Exodus 33:18.
3. John 20:11-17.
4. John 20:27.
5. Leviticus 16:17.
6. Hebrews 12:24.
7. See Ephesians 4:11.
8. Exodus 17:6.
9. Numbers 20:7-11.
10. Hebrews 9:26b.
11. Exodus 30:23-25.
12. I Thessalonians 5:18.
13. Exodus 37:29.
14. See Leviticus 6:12-13.
15. Matthew 18:18.
16. Proverbs 30:19.

Chapter 2

The Anointing and Sanctification

In the beginning God created the heaven and the earth. And the earth was without form, and void; and darkness was upon the face of the deep. And the Spirit of God moved upon the face of the waters.

Genesis 1:1-2

Deep calleth unto deep at the noise of Thy waterspouts: all Thy waves and Thy billows are gone over me.

Psalm 42:7

A waterspout is the pressure of air on the face of water. Water is a type of humanity. The force of air is a type of the Spirit. As God moved upon the face of the waters, so He moves upon humanity. One reason He moves upon humanity is to call them to prayer. He moves on us and gives the call to prayer.

There is a transmission, a frequency of announcement, in God. There is a place where God is always speaking, always calling. "Deep calleth unto deep...." We cannot come to God, however, without a spiritual drawing up to Him.

> *No man can come to Me, except the Father which hath
> sent Me draw him.*

> John 6:44a

When deep calls, He does not call to height. He does not
call to width. Deep does not call to breadth.

> [That you] *may be able to comprehend with all saints
> what is the breadth, and length, and depth, and height;
> and to know the love of Christ, which passeth knowledge,
> that ye might be filled with all the fulness of God.*

> Ephesians 3:18-19

If deep calls to deep, and God calls on the frequency that
is deep, then we must respond on the same frequency. If, for
example, I am always tuned to height, and God calls depth, I
will not hear Him. If God is talking on channel 4, and I am
listening on channel 10, I may hear a lot of junk, but I will
not hear God. So we must learn to flip our dial. God talks on
more than one frequency.

Sometimes God speaks in high and holy praise and worship. He weighs the hearts of all men. He knows the balance
of the spirit. He knows where you and I fall behind.

Discover the height, the depth and the width so when the
Spirit of God moves on the face of the waters and God comes
out to touch you, you will know Him in the heights and the
depths. If He calls the deep, you can answer on deep. If He
calls the height, you can answer on height. You need to know
Him in every dimension of the spirit.

Flowing From the Height

There are depths of spiritual operation. The anointing has
many levels. It is not just an allotment of spiritual goods that
God pours out on His people. There are divine channels that

have depth and width according to the purpose carved out, by sanctification, in our individual lives.

Behold, how good and how pleasant it is for brethren to dwell together in unity! It is like the precious ointment upon the head, that ran down upon the beard, even Aaron's beard: that went down to the skirts of his garments; as the dew of Hermon, and as the dew that descended upon the mountains of Zion: for there the Lord commanded the blessing, even life for evermore.

Psalm 133

The anointing is like water. The anointing flows down like the waters from the mountains. So the anointing in our lives is related to the height and the depth.

The height of the mountains determines the depth of the rivers because the volume of moisture in the snow and the rain that the mountain can absorb pours out into the springs, tributaries, brooks and creeks. All that water finds its way to the lowest point between the mountains to the major water course.

I cannot go from where I live in upstate New York to Long Island without crossing the major water course that drains the Adirondack forest (50 million acres) and the Catskills. In the Adirondacks, there are 44 peaks over 4,000 feet high. They loom and overshadow you as they cast their breadths across the freeway when you drive to Albany. All the ice, snow, water and springs from these peaks empty into one major water course called the Hudson River. The Hudson River is deep enough for the ships that come from all over the world to travel to the major port of Albany, all because the mountains catch the dew and the waters of the heavens.

So I myself want to know all about the geometry of the anointing. I need to know the complexity of that equation. I am not satisfied to be a shallow marsh. I am not happy to simply contain moisture. It does not satisfy me to be some snowflake sprinkled on a barren field. I want to be more than a drizzle in the Kingdom of God. I would like to be a part of a downpour. I would like to be an artesian well. I want more than just average, mundane Christianity. I need a Holy Ghost baptism!

The anointing oil, representing the anointing, was a precious ointment. Things that are precious are rare. Some metals are more valuable than others because they cannot be found along the highway or around a junkyard. Men give their lives, lose their wives, and give their children and fortunes for the possibility of finding one golden nugget in the bottom of a mountain stream, simply because it is rare.

The Psalmist also said that it was "good" and "pleasant." The word *pleasant* in Hebrew means "something of rare finding." It is like a breath alone. It is like finding something unique and singular. It is pleasant for brethren to dwell together in unity. It is like the precious ointment upon the head that ran down upon the beard.

The anointing always flows down. Did you ever see a river flow up? One time I was driving along where the river and the road were side by side on the mountain. It looked like the water was going uphill. I was completely certain that the water was flowing upstream. I even stopped my car to go look at it. However, where the road carved the side of the mountain, the direction the water traveled was still down. The water always flows down. The water never flows to the top of the mountain to run over and go to the other side.

The water flows down the mountains through the river's courses. In the springtime when the ice and snow melts, the water in the New York area flows to the Hudson River, where the main water course meets the lowest point of resistance of the land. The water will flow down around the roots of the trees, down through the moist ferns, down through the spring lilies, and down into the gulches and gullies. The water flows down into the brooks and the creeks and down to the river. The water flows down.

As a man stands before you, the highest part of his stature is his head. Man does not walk on his head and put his feet up in the air. So if you had anointed Aaron with a horn of oil, the oil would pour down over his beard and his garments, all the way down to the skirts of his garments. The anointing flows down.

The anointing is also like the dew of Hermon. The Psalmist uses the name of Hermon in this passage because it is a high mountain. Hermon is not just a little hill. Here the water does not come up out of the earth as dew normally covers the fields. The morning dew comes up, but the dew of Hermon descends.

Similarly, the anointing must come upon us at the highest point of our experience. The anointing first touches what we raise the highest to God in our life.

Sanctification Flows Up

In order to raise up the mountain of possibility in your life, in order to become the collective source and to gather more of the flowing of the Spirit, there must be something that starts from the foot and goes up. It is called sanctification. While anointing flows down, sanctification flows up. If we do not put those two things together, simultaneously, there is a danger in anointing the unsanctified.

What are preachers? You can give them license papers and certificates of ordination for 40 bucks. Paper mills turn out attractively arrayed, ruffled papers with crimped gold stars on their left corners, signed by no-named nothings who never felt a touch of God and who never knew His power. Sometimes credentials have a stronger relationship to ink, paper and printing presses than they have to the power of prayer and the purpose of God.

The Scriptures instruct us to lay hands suddenly on no man.[1] If you are a man of God and part of a gathering of powerful, anointed men, you cannot just lay hands on everybody. You might become a partaker of other men's sin. If you lay your hands on the unsanctified, you give authority to their uncleanness.

We need God to lay His hand on us. If He anoints us, He will anoint our head. The anointing must, however, come from something first pressed upward toward Him so the anointing can flow downward, even to the hems of the garments.

And this is the thing that thou shalt do unto them to hallow them, to minister unto Me in the priest's office.

Exodus 29:1a

The anointing is for priests as well as for kings. That's what we are to the Lord; we are kings and priests unto our God.2 We are not just patrons of a certain faith. We have not simply come into religion. When God called us in this great era of grace, He called us to be kings and priests unto Him.

As such you offer sacrifices of praise. Your conversion and redemptive responsibility is one of offering gifts. So offer up unto Him the gifts of praise. As for sacrifices, the Psalmist says, "I will offer to Thee the sacrifice of thanksgiving."[3] Yet there is still another offering. It is not of yourself to God, but of yourself for God.

It is wonderful for us to be able to participate in our redemptive responsibility by offering praises and sacrifices of love to the Lord, but if we ever intend to make an impact in priesthood, in the work of God, in order to do more than edify ourselves, there is an extra measure of sanctification and consecration that we need. That extra measure takes us out of the average Christianity that seeks personal, spiritual gratification and launches us into a kingdom-consciousness. We must constantly pray, "Not as I will, but as You will. It is not what I want that is important, but what You want. It is not where I will be that counts, but where You would have me to be." That is the prayer that takes us away from ourselves. That prayer crucifies flesh and ambition. It is death to self-will. It destroys egocentric people. It messes up people who live for themselves. It is called sanctification.

And the very God of peace sanctify you wholly; and I pray God your whole spirit and soul and body be preserved blameless unto the coming of our Lord Jesus Christ.

I Thessalonians 5:23

We should become so totally lost in the purpose of Calvary that we no longer seek our own. We need to find the highest purpose.

Starting at the Bottom

The Hermon in your life needs to reach all the way into the clouds in order that, wherever an anointing hits, your peak is the first to gather water. You need your river to be deep in God. You need the base of your mountain to be broad.

How does a mountain get a broad base? The upheavals in the earth blow up and form mountains. Fault lines in the crust of the earth move and twist the stones and rocks. Scientists tell us that through billions (or trillions) of years the earth has undergone one cataclysmic eruption after another. That is what formed the rocks. Rocks stand up along the highways where passes were cut through the mountains for the road. According to science, powerful inner-earth pressures pushed up the mountains. As in volcanos, fires erupt deep in the heart of the earth to produce mountains. That boiling lava is so hot, the crust of the earth can no longer be content to lie level and flat. The earth starts heaving and blows like Mount St. Helens. It throws dust, dirt, trees and lava for miles. It brings devastation to the living things on the mountain.

Sanctification does not start at the top of the mountain and come down. Sanctification starts with a boiling fire inside your earth that will not let you remain normal and flat. Sanctification starts out feeling something like, "I must have a place in God." It is fueled by another message, another song, and another mandate until, suddenly, there is that holy eruption. Somewhere in the back of the choir or from the corner of the auditorium you cannot take it any more. "Whatever it takes, I have to get out of myself and into God." Desire like a holy fire boils out until it creates the mountain in your life. It becomes a water flow for cascading spiritual moisture, a Hermon for the dew of anointing to fall on, something on top of you that makes a headship for God to anoint. It can flow down to the valleys, fill up the oceans, and give life to the earth.

What else begins at the bottom, like sanctification?

And Aaron and his sons thou shalt bring unto the door of the tabernacle of the congregation, and shalt wash them with water. And thou shalt take the garments, and put upon Aaron the coat, and the robe of the ephod, and the ephod, and the breastplate, and gird him with the curious girdle of the ephod: and thou shalt put the mitre upon his head, and put the holy crown upon the mitre.

Exodus 29:4-6

The dressing of the priest begins with his "britches." "Britches" is not just a Texas word, it is also a Holy Ghost word. You must put "britches" on the priest. "Britches" are undergarments. They start at the ankle and go up the thigh to the waist. Then you put on the robe, the coat, the breastplate, the mitre, and the crown. Dressing the priest for anointing does not start with the ephod and go down. Dressing the priest starts at the foot and goes up. So whatever you pour anointing oil on, make sure it had sanctification start at the foot and go up.

Jesus did a strange thing too. Just before He died, He rose up from the table and girded Himself with a towel. Jesus went *down* and began to wash their feet. Sanctification always begins at the feet. He could have anointed the head, but instead He washed their feet. Feisty Simon said, "Do You, Lord, wash my feet?" Jesus looked at him and said, "You do not know what I am doing now. You do not understand it. You will know hereafter."[4]

The Church never learned it hereafter. The Church does not know what Jesus did there. He said, "If I don't wash you, Simon, you have no part with Me." Simon Peter, when a little Hebrew boy, knew something of Moses. So Peter did more than just throw out a few ideas about blessings placed upon his appendages. He laid himself over the tabernacle and said, "Not my feet only, but my hands and my head also. Wash me all the way from my feet to my head."[5]

Although the anointing flows down, the washing of the water by the Word needs to flow up from our feet.[6] If we cannot start with the anointing in the realm of the servant, we have no right to live in the honor of kings and priests.

The Door to the Priesthood

If you want to be a priest, you must start at the door. Aaron did not get dressed on the corner or around at the back of the tabernacle. The priests did not boost Aaron up and throw him over the fence to let him run in, lift up the curtain to jump in, and say, "I am in the Holy of Holies! I am in here where the glory is." If you want head realm in the stature of Christ, you must come through the door.

At the door of the tabernacle there was a brass altar. That is the altar of death. Everything died at the brazen altar. The brazen altar was a type of the flesh. You must destroy your own will. Sanctification starts at the brass altar with death to flesh and self and with judgment against sin.

There was another piece of furniture there also, called the brazen laver. It had water in it for the cleansing of the priest.

After you pass the brazen furniture of the altar and the laver, you go into a little tent (made out of badger skins and ram skins dyed red) called the Holy Place. Three pieces of furniture stood in the Holy Place. There were the seven candlesticks, a little table for showbread that the priest baked and put on it, and a little altar 18 inches by 18 inches by 36 inches high, called the golden altar, on which the incense was burned.

Once a year, in the depths beyond the Holy Place, the high priest went inside the veil to the holiest of all, the inner sanctum sanctorium. There the glory of God lived between the cherubim over the mercy seat of the ark of the covenant.

If you lay a cross over the top of the arrangement of furniture, the brazen altar was set at the foot where men nailed Christ's feet to the cross. There both blood and water flowed from Christ's side. Both of those elements were in the laver. In the Holy Place, there were candlesticks and showbread. So the heart of God is worship and praise. The glory and the headship were at the ark of the covenant. All these things in the tabernacle were types depicting Christ.

In which realm in Christ does sanctification begin? Your feet! The door is down there! Do you want to begin into ministry? You must start down there! Do you want to work for God? Do you want your mountain to be full of dew? There will not be any mountain unless you start with a fire in your earth that pushes and blows up and says, "I want to raise up something in my life that God can anoint."

End Notes

1. I Timothy 5:22.
2. Revelation 1:6.
3. Psalm 116:17a.
4. John 13:2-7.
5. John 13:8-9.
6. Ephesians 5:26.

Chapter 3

The Covering for Ministry

The clothing of the priest is extremely important to the anointing. In fact, the son of the priest could not become priest unless he wore his father's priestly garments for seven days.

And the holy garments of Aaron shall be his sons' after him, to be anointed therein, and to be consecrated in them. And that son that is priest in his stead shall put them on seven days, when he cometh into the tabernacle of the congregation to minister in the holy place.

Exodus 29:29-30

The Priestly Garments

And take thou unto thee Aaron thy brother, and his sons with him, from among the children of Israel, that he may minister unto Me in the priest's office, even Aaron, Nadab and Abihu, Eleazar and Ithamar, Aaron's sons. And thou shalt make holy garments for Aaron thy brother for glory and for beauty. And thou shalt speak unto all that are wise hearted, whom I have filled with the spirit of wisdom, that they may make Aaron's garments to consecrate him, that he may minister unto Me in the priest's office. And these are the garments which they shall make; a breastplate, and an ephod, and a robe, and a broidered coat, a mitre, and a girdle: and they shall make holy garments for Aaron thy brother, and his sons, that he may minister unto Me in the priest's office.

Exodus 28:1-4

Every piece of the priest's clothing represented something spiritual. These garments were made with the embroidery of gold, blue and purple. The mitre was a gold band worn on top of the head. The mitre represents holiness to the Lord. The breastplate of righteousness had 12 stones set in it. Each stone represented one tribe of Israel under the Urim and the Thummim. We might call it a stoplight or a go light. It was a yes or a no. It was the answer of the Holy Spirit over the heart of the priest. Other stones were set on the shoulders of the garment; they listed the names of the tribes of Israel. Thus the priests carried on their shoulders the hearts of the tribes of Israel. The skirt of the garment was bordered with pomegranates, which represents the provision of God. The bells also went all the way around the hem and had a very eminent purpose. If the high priest went into the Holy of Holies, the ringing of the bells signaled to those outside the veil that God had received the sacrifice and the high priest was still alive. If they did not hear the ringing of the bells, they knew that the sacrifice had not been received and the high priest was dead.

The passage also says that these garments were made by the "wise-hearted." God told Moses, "I want you to speak to the people, to all who are wise-hearted, and tell them that they are to make clothes for the priests." Those garments were for Aaron and his sons to be anointed and consecrated in. So wise-hearted people make garments for ministry.

The Old Testament Scriptures describe them as physical garments worn on the shoulders and bodies of men. But in the New Testament, they are spiritual garments. They are not just physical garments. So if we are wise-hearted, we will clothe each other.

Spiritual Garments

The Spirit of the Lord God is upon Me; because the Lord hath anointed Me... To appoint unto them that mourn in Zion, to give unto them beauty for ashes, the oil of joy for mourning, the garment of praise for the spirit of heaviness; that they might be called trees of righteousness, the planting of the Lord, that He might be glorified.

Isaiah 61:1,3

The garments of spiritual life are garments that are weaved with words. We put on the garments of praise for the spirit of heaviness. These garments are put on us by words that are spoken. They are weaved by terminologies. Expressed ideas color them. If we put on garments of praise, then they must be garments created by praise.

Let the words of my mouth, and the meditation of my heart, be acceptable in Thy sight, O Lord, my strength, and my redeemer.

Psalm 19:14

Let Thy priests be clothed with righteousness; and let Thy saints shout for joy.

Psalm 132:9

I will also clothe her priests with salvation: and her saints shall shout aloud for joy.

Psalm 132:16

I will greatly rejoice in the Lord, my soul shall be joyful in my God; for He hath clothed me with the garments of salvation, He hath covered me with the robe of righteousness, as a bridegroom decketh himself with ornaments, and as a bride adorneth herself with her jewels.

Isaiah 61:10

If we desire to have the house of God melt together, then we must overcome our tendency to become islands unto ourselves. Those who are wise-hearted have learned that, if they make the proper coats of praise, worship, giving and consecration, all the priests will look alike. Nobody is higher than anybody else. No one is more important than another. Every house in its uniqueness has a gifted vision that is not necessarily like another's was, is or will be. But if we live in one house, we need to have its vision. We speak where we can agree. We come into agreement where we can come into agreement. If we do not agree, then we refrain from speaking.

Death and life are in the power of the tongue: and they that love it shall eat the fruit thereof.

Proverbs 18:21

My soul is among lions: and I lie even among them that are set on fire, even the sons of men, whose teeth are spears and arrows, and their tongue a sharp sword.

Psalm 57:4

I can build a haven for your heart with my mouth or I can use my tongue as a sharp sword, piercing the inner spirit. I can have a sharp tongue and pierce a person's inner spirit. Yet I can take the same needle that stabbed the heart with pain and weave a garment of love. It takes wise people to make these garments.

As an example, consider Noah after the flood. I personally do not think that Noah knew what the grapes would do to him, but he became drunk. He had left the ark and planted a vineyard. He made himself drunk on his own success. Then he was lying in his tent, unconscious and naked. Without wisdom, his middle son, Ham, looked into the tent.[1]

There are two Hebrew words that you need to learn here.

1. *Raah.* Ham *saw* his father naked. He looked at his father and saw the situation.

2. *Nagad.* He *told* his brethren what happened.

What did Ham do that was so bad? Ham saw his son with his unconscious and naked father and he told his brothers. When Noah woke up, he "knew what his younger son [in Hebrew, littlest male or grandson] had done unto him."[2] He then cursed Ham's fourth son, Canaan.

What is the big deal about Ham? Study the two words. *Raah* means "to look upon with delight." When Ham looked at his father, it pleased him that his father had been abused. *Nagad* means that "he told it with a hilarious feeling." It excited Ham to tell his brothers. *Raah*—he looked with satisfaction. *Nagad*—he told it with delight. It sounds simple when you say, "He saw his father naked and he told his brothers." But, "He stared as his father was sexually abused. He told his brothers very delightedly," presents a bad spirit. Ham's son carried the curse (and still does to this day), and Ham's brothers carried the blessing.

Ham was willing to leave his father uncovered. When his two brothers found their father unclothed, they backed into the tent with a garment. They would not even look. They covered his iniquity.[3]

That should be our attitude toward the pain other people have in their lives. We should never look with satisfaction and tell it with delight. We should always back up to cover people and say, "I love you." Let's put some garments on them. We create that coat of clothing with our mouths.

And the angel came in unto her, and said, Hail, thou that art highly favoured, the Lord is with thee: blessed art thou among women. And when she saw him, she was troubled at his saying, and cast in her mind what manner of salutation this should be.

Luke 1:28-29

The angel came to tell Mary that she would have a baby. "Hail, you are highly favored. You are blessed among women." Mary cast about in her mind the nature of the salutation. "The Lord is with you. You are blessed among women."

And Mary arose in those days, and went into the hill country with haste, into a city of Juda; and entered into the house of Zacharias, and saluted Elisabeth. And it came to pass, that, when Elisabeth heard the salutation of Mary, the babe leaped in her womb; and Elisabeth was filled with the Holy Ghost: and she spake out with a loud voice, and said, Blessed art thou among women, and blessed is the fruit of thy womb.

Luke 1:39-42

Mary went into the mountains. She met with Elisabeth, her cousin, who was expecting a baby. When Mary went into the house, she "saluted Elisabeth."

The salutation the angel gave Mary clothed her. She went into the mountains and found her cousin Elisabeth. Mary took the same coat the angel gave her and put it on Elisabeth. "The Lord is with you." Then Elisabeth said, "The moment the voice of your salutation sounded in my ear, my baby, my dream, my hope and my possibility, leaped in my womb."[4] For six months Elisabeth's baby had not moved. For six months he seemed lifeless in the womb. For six months nothing happened until Mary believed what God told her and she told it to Elisabeth. It was the communication of faith. When the baby leaped, Elisabeth said, "Blessed is she who believed, for now there shall be a fulfillment of that word spoken by the word of the Lord."[5]

Why did the baby jump when Mary addressed Elisabeth, and not before? If Mary had not believed the angel, there would not have been a Jesus. If there had not been a Jesus, there would be no need for John the Baptist. When someone else believed what God told her and communicated that to Elisabeth, it made Elisabeth's dream come true. All our dreams depend on what somebody else around us is hearing from God.

When we become a congregation of segregated people, one where everyone has separate ideas, dreams, futures and zeals, then we only stop over in the same watering hole and never fulfill one another's visions or clothe one another's dreams. All we do is sing to each other, satisfy each other for the moment, and wave goodbye while we all scatter and go other places as soon as we can. If we have a longevity and a purpose in God, then I hold something that will make your baby jump. You hold something that will make someone else's baby jump. If we truly want to hear what God has to say about our life, we need to start making clothes for other people. When others get anointed, they may say something back to us that makes our dream come into focus.

Let what comes out of your mouth go into the weaver's fashion in such a way that it lays upon whomever it falls as a garment that anoints and consecrates him. It is impossible to anoint someone in the house of God when you have just filled his ears with gossip.

Covering Iniquity

He that covereth his sins shall not prosper: but whoso confesseth and forsaketh them shall have mercy.

Proverbs 28:13

If a person covers his sins, he shall not prosper. This verse refers to the one who sins. If he covers his sin, he will not prosper, unless he repents. If he repents and makes it right, God will bless him.

Hatred stirreth up strifes: but love covereth all sins.

Proverbs 10:12

Proverbs 10:12 seems to contradict Proverbs 28:13. Both verses speak of covering sins. The person to cover the sin, however, is not the person who committed the sin. If somebody commits sin against God, he is personally responsible for making it right. Anyone around the sinner, who senses something wrong in him, should not expose his ungodly living. We should not stand around waiting for someone to do something wrong so we can reveal that iniquity. The word *cover* in Proverbs 10:12 does not mean "to hide." It means "to cover with a garment."

When I find somebody who is suffering, who has done wrong or who has committed something out of line, if I am wise, I will cover that iniquity. That does not mean I should hide it, but God gives me no right to expose it either. God gives me the wise heart to make a garment to anoint and consecrate the offender.

The Church must learn that the headship and eldership is responsible for correction in the house of God. It is not right that every saint of God has become a watchdog eyeing everybody else. When we do that, something is wrong with everybody.

When we say, "Brother, I do not agree with what you are doing," we immediately tend not just to uncover sin, but also to watch, criticize and judge. That tendency is eating up the Christian church. Congregations watch, waiting for someone to make a wrong move. Rumors of sin and problems in the church fly around everywhere. People criticize families because of certain things that happen to other family members. It becomes very easy to talk about the failings of people. It is just like the racial bigotry in this nation.

Churches also tend to create caste systems. "They came from over there at the Assembly of God church." "He used to be in Virginia." "He came from New York out on the island." "Their church blew up so he came hiding over here." We tend to put people in slots.

Ignorance in the congregation then becomes a cesspool of gossip and chatter. Wisdom in the congregation, however, knows better than to try to pinpoint everyone's problem. God's grace is greater than our judgment. God is able by the Holy Spirit to convict of sin. He does not need us to point out everyone's problem. But if we can produce enough glory in the house, the unrighteous cannot sit in the congregation of the righteous.

> ***Therefore the ungodly shall not stand in the judgment, nor sinners in the congregation of the righteous.***
>
> Psalm 1:5

Judgment also will I lay to the line, and righteousness to the plummet: and the hail shall sweep away the refuge of lies, and the waters shall overflow the hiding place.

Isaiah 28:17

My responsibility in the Church is not to find out what is right or wrong. My responsibility is to produce so much of the glory of God in the house that the rising tide uncovers the hiding place. He said, "I will lay judgment to the line, and righteousness to the plummet. I will line up everything." If the Church needs holiness, what will you do about it? Will you talk to everyone about it until you make everyone mad? Or are you willing to start producing enough of the glory of God that the waters overflow the hiding place? When the water rises high enough, the varmints, the snakes and the muskrats start crawling out on the banks.

If you want your church to be holy, you need to make coats so everybody in the house can be anointed and consecrated. You yourself can help produce holiness and bring the church into righteousness. That does not mean you are the preacher or the judge. Rather, it is for everyone to participate in the work of the Levite, who in wisdom says, "I will start making garments. I will make coats for Aaron, my pastors, my elders, and sons. I will make coats for everybody in the church. I will do what God did." The very first act God did for man, after the fall, was to become man's tailor.

God became a tailor. He made coats for people who had sinned against Him. He made a way for them to be covered. It required the sacrifice of a part of His creation, a part that He had fashioned and provided with life. He took away life in order to cover man, so man could live. When Adam and Eve walked out of that garden, fig leaves did not cover them. Their clothing cost a sacrifice.

Unto Adam also and to his wife did the Lord God make coats of skins, and clothed them.

Genesis 3:21

The very first thing God did concerning man after man had sinned was to shed the blood of an animal. You may say, "He was shedding blood for their sin." That is true. God shed blood for a covering of skins. The blood was shed to provide a covering. Blood was not shed merely so blood would be shed. God shed blood because He desired to cover their iniquity with the skins of animals. Something had to die to provide a covering.

Jesus did not die simply to shed blood. He shed blood to robe us in His righteousness. He died to provide a covering for us. He shed blood to save us and give us right standing with God. We can say, "I am redeemed by blood divine." The love of God did this great work.

The Garments to Remove

It is hard for a church with many people from many squadrons with many abilities and talents from many places with many ideas and feelings and different hopes and dreams to melt together. Churches tend to become sideshows for a presentation of talents. People pick out which ones they like. "I enjoyed the songs this morning, except for one. I hope they do not sing that one for awhile."

We all hold such reservations. It is like putting on a shirt but no pants. It is like going to town without a shirt on. You have seen the sign: NO SHIRT. NO SHOES. NO SERVICE. We need to hang that sign in the house of God. Everyone in the service needs to remove whatever and whoever he is. In the house of God, we are just worshipers.

And David was clothed with a robe of fine linen, and all the Levites that bare the ark, and the singers, and Chenaniah the master of the song with the singers: David also had upon him an ephod of linen. Thus all Israel brought up the ark of the covenant of the Lord with shouting, and with sound of the cornet, and with trumpets, and with cymbals, making a noise with psalteries and harps. And it came to pass, as the ark of the covenant of the Lord came to the city of David, that Michal the daughter of Saul looking out at a window saw king David dancing and playing: and she despised him in her heart.

I Chronicles 15:27-29

Then David returned to bless his household. And Michal the daughter of Saul came out to meet David, and said, How glorious was the king of Israel today, who uncovered himself today in the eyes of the handmaids of his servants, as one of the vain fellows shamelessly uncovereth himself! And David said unto Michal, It was before the Lord, which chose me before thy father, and before all his house, to appoint me ruler over the people of the Lord, over Israel: therefore will I play before the Lord. And I will yet be more vile than thus, and will be base in mine own sight: and of the maidservants which thou hast spoken of, of them shall I be had in honour. Therefore Michal the daughter of Saul had no child unto the day of her death.

II Samuel 6:20-23

David danced before the Lord wearing a priest's ephod. His carnal wife accused him of nakedness. She said, "Oh, the king was magnificent today when he danced naked before all the maidens of Israel. Did you enjoy yourself?" David was not naked. He wore the priest's garments. He wore a covering, but it was not the covering of the king's robe. Michal liked him as a king. She hated him as a worshiper. She wanted him with a crown and a scepter, and with gold. She did not desire him to be a praiser, a dancer or a worshiper. So when we come into the house of God, we need to remove something.

And they came to Jericho: and as He went out of Jericho with His disciples and a great number of people, blind Bartimaeus, the son of Timaeus, sat by the highway side begging. And when he heard that it was Jesus of Nazareth, he began to cry out, and say, Jesus, Thou son of David, have mercy on me. And many charged him that he should hold his peace: but he cried the more a great deal, Thou son of David, have mercy on me. And Jesus stood still, and commanded him to be called. And they call the blind man, saying unto him, Be of good comfort, rise; He calleth thee. And he, casting away his garment, rose, and came to Jesus. And Jesus answered and said unto him, What wilt thou that I should do unto thee? The blind man said unto Him, Lord, that I might receive my sight. And Jesus said unto him, Go thy way; thy faith hath made thee whole. And immediately he received his sight, and followed Jesus in the way.

Mark 10:46-52

The blind man sat begging, "Jesus, have mercy on me." Jesus said, "Bring him to Me." When the blind man stood, he threw off his garments. He came to Jesus without his own identity. There needs to be a great loss of personal identities. We need to lose our identities in the greater vision of unity of purpose. Then we can cover everyone around us with garments to anoint and consecrate them.

Too many of us wait for our dreams and hopes to come to pass. We look for direction. We look for somebody to ask us to go somewhere. We should lose the uncharted ambition that makes us so restless. It makes us impatient for something we can never obtain. Impatience never receives an answer. We will not find the ultimate purpose of our life and ministry by chafing at the bit.

You say, "But Brother Mark, I want to know what God has for me." Why not shut up for awhile and enjoy where you are at? For me, it makes no difference what I am, what I have been, or what I think I will be. I need to ignore and lose whatever revelations I have that a local church seems to oppose while God has me in that church. I ought to bury myself in the purpose of the dream of that particular house. It does not matter whether I have less or more gifting than that of the administrative head of the church. God did not put me there because I have less or more than the leadership. God does not put me in a place to be under somebody of greater of lesser abilities. Whomever God puts over me, his wisdom, his years of experience, his background, his magnificence, or even his smallness, has nothing to do with my submission. My submission is not given because I have found someone greater. My submission is given because I am great enough in my spirit to cover whatever headship God gives me.

I have learned that, in wisdom, I make garments for the priests who worship with me. That is how we are anointed. That is where I find my answers. I receive my answers because somebody else, in turn, makes me a coat. Even though I have been preaching for 30 years, I pray that people will take that tongue God has given them and say, "Brother Mark, do you know that God has His hand on your life? He will use you. You are in this place for proving and testing. If God was not trying to work something out in your life, you would not be here, would you, Brother Mark?" We can sew someone a fine coat like that. Let's take our tongue and weave something that is full of faith and encouragement.

For we have great joy and consolation in thy love, because the bowels of the saints are refreshed by thee, brother.

Philemon 7

Paul said to Philemon, "Brother, you have just encouraged the bowels of the saints." The word *bowels* means "everything inside me." My bowels are my heart, my spirit, my insecurities and my needs. Regardless of my gifting and talent, I need somebody to encourage me inside my spirit. Somebody can always say, "Hi! How are you doing?" That is not what I need. I need somebody to say, "Brother, God is with you." Say it twice. Sew up the other sleeve. So if we fail to make these garments for each other, we leave people naked in their loneliness, struggling in their seeming insignificance, and hurting in their misdirection until they just sit, chafe, stew and wonder why.

Clothing for the Anointing

An atmosphere of anointing does not do you any good if it is poured on without clothes. You cannot receive it. You go home and there is nothing to hold the odor of the oil. Nothing is holding the substance. In the morning that anointing is gone and loneliness returns. The bruise is back again. The emptiness is still there because the anointing fails to linger.

Clothe people so the next time anointing falls, the aroma hangs in their clothes. The next morning when they go to work, they still smell it. The next day when they come home, it is still lingering. That's why we need to clothe one another with our words.

My mother used to have a small bottle of perfume that my oldest sister had sent her. It was a very small bottle that she kept for years. Every so often mother would pour a little bit on the edge of her handkerchief. "Momma, why are you doing that?" I would ask. She said, "Honey, this is real perfume that my daughter bought for me." "Why not just put it on you?" I asked. She said, "On me?" I said, "On you. Just put it on you, so it would stay on you." She said, "Oh, no. You need to put it on something that it can soak into, and saturate. If you want it to linger, it must have something to get hold of. If I just put it on me, the next time I took a bath, it would no longer be there. I carry this little handkerchief with me, and it just stays and stays."

The anointing disappears with your morning tears because there is no coat to hold it. That is how the anointing is lost. We need to start saying good things to each other. We need to start encouraging one another. Will the world encourage us? Will the devil make us feel good? Let's begin to build up one another.

But ye, beloved, building up yourselves on your most holy faith, praying in the Holy Ghost.

Jude 20

What do I do when I become full of the Holy Ghost and am built up? I make something for someone else. "I was in prayer this morning and the Lord told me that He will take your gifting and talent and use it in the four corners of the earth. The music and melody of your spirit will go far and wide. It will be seen, heard, touched and felt. God will greatly use you."

Getting the Anointing

You say you want an anointing. You can have it right now. In fact, it is on you now. Do you know where it came from? It did not come down. It came out. You are a priest. You are a Levite. You have a wise heart. You produce anointing. You make coats to put on others.

The gifting God has given you is more than a small thing in a local church. God will raise it up and glorify Himself through you. It does not have to be prophecy. It is just a word spoken in due season. Say the right thing at the right time. The Holy Ghost should usher it in, and the Spirit should state it.

Sometimes the things I need so much to make my dream and vision live are locked in the heart and mouth of someone else in my world. I am trying to obtain it from God. But someone else can very well hold the key and the answer to what I am waiting for God to give me.

Have you ever had problems? Have you ever done wrong? Were you ever bad? Is there anything in your life that you want to hide? Did you repent? Did God forgive you? Are you worthy to preach? He made me worthy. He is worthy, and I am in Him. He made me a coat. As long as I wear the coat, I can preach.

If you dig around and uncover me, I lose my anointing. I would not be worthy to preach because you would lose the value of my message, knowing the pain of my past. If you clothe me and pour oil on me, though, you and I can both be anointed. We can be children of God.

Please do not remove my coat. Do not take your tongue and cut the buttons from the pastor's shirt. Refuse to take your tongue and speak against the embellished praise of the ministry.

We need to let the mind of unity become like the anointing oil. "Behold, how good and pleasant it is for brethren to dwell together in unity! It is like the precious ointment...."[6] We need to learn that if we reach up and pour oil on the headship, it will flow down and catch us on its way down. If we make garments for others, we prepare ourselves to receive a coat from somebody else.

End Notes

1. Genesis 9:20-22.
2. Genesis 9:24.
3. Genesis 9:23.
4. Luke 1:44.
5. Luke 1:45.
6. Psalm 133:1-2.

Chapter 4

The Order of Aaron

There is something very, very special that God wants to say to us about our relationships with one another.

First, I thank my God through Jesus Christ for you all, that your faith is spoken of throughout the whole world. For God is my witness, whom I serve with my spirit in the gospel of His Son, that without ceasing I make mention of you always in my prayers; making request, if by any means now at length I might have a prosperous journey by the will of God to come unto you. For I long to see you, that I may impart unto you some spiritual gift, to the end ye may be established; that is, that I may be comforted together with you by the mutual faith both of you and me.

Romans 1:8-12

The word *established*, in this instance, does not mean just "learning doctrine," but "finding comfort." "Establishing" is coming into proper relationship. The apostle is saying, "I want to impart something to you that we might come into proper relationship."

We need so desperately to find ourselves in relationships. Separating ourselves to God and to the work of God often causes us to become isolated. Sometimes those of us in ministry isolate ourselves. After all, God calls us from among our brethren when we enter into ministry. Then we find ourselves isolated. We are suddenly alone.

Members of a congregation have an advantage over preachers and others in the ministry. A member in a congregation has brothers, sisters, friends and certain relatives with whom to eat and visit in the home. The congregation becomes an association of friends.

Sometimes, when we are in our own ministry, we do not have as many friends as we had in the congregation. Many times our friends are our peers. Some of our friends may be pastors of larger churches, pastors of smaller ones, and others who are not pastoring yet. Some of our friends may minister in the streets. Some are intercessors. As ministers, we try to find levels in which we can fellowship. Yet we may still float hopelessly about, wondering where we are, who we are, and if we are.

We need proper relationships. But how do we find these relationships? Where do they come from?

Spiritual Impartation

There is a doctrine of the New Testament called the doctrine of spiritual impartation. Spiritual impartation comes primarily by the laying on of hands. The laying on of hands, the thing that directs you into a ministry, is also an ordination. That is the pattern of which the Old Testament presents a type. But has the Church followed this pattern?

I have travelled the country for years and I have watched ministries. I have observed the anemic preaching trying to evangelize the world. I have watched men depart from churches to begin other works. I have watched men start new works in certain areas and the swarming of the bees as they gathered a new queen. I have watched the evangelists, the young preachers, stomping in the field trying to reap a little harvest as they emulate the operation of what the pastor and the church should be doing all the time. We have turned the evangelistic field into a place for new preachers to try to find a church to pastor. We have turned cities into pincushions, places to throw our preaching darts to make a score.

Many times men establish churches because of division. Someone starts a church down the street or across town because he did not like what was happening in the church he previously attended. Suddenly, he feels led to start a church. "God spoke to him" because he did not like the correction that the pastor gave him. "God spoke to him" to go to the next town and take three families and start another work.

This action has been common, especially in the Pentecostal church, for as long as it has existed. But it is so much against Scripture and against Christ that it is no mystery our works average small numbers. It is not surprising that large churches are not common among our ranks.

We have not put apostolic ministry into the field. We have not put prophetic and anointed men into the field. We put splinter groups and shavings of what was once a beautiful piece of ministerial furniture out somewhere to do the work of God without the glorious advantage of the approval of the Holy Ghost.

For every high priest taken from among men is ordained for men in things pertaining to God, that he may offer both gifts and sacrifices for sins: who can have compassion on the ignorant, and on them that are out of the way; for that he himself also is compassed with infirmity. And by reason hereof he ought, as for the people, so also for himself, to offer for sins. And no man taketh this honour unto himself, but he that is called of God, as was Aaron. So also Christ glorified not Himself to be made an high priest; but He that said unto Him, Thou art My Son, to day have I begotten Thee.

Hebrews 5:1-5

No man takes the honor of priesthood or of being an high priest. The high priest directs other priests. The Church is a nation of priests. God calls high priests who are able to care for those who are out of the way. These priests must, by reason of infirmity, have learned to care for the weak and the hurting. But they cannot take this honor to themselves. They must be called of God, as was Aaron.

It is no secret that we have not followed the order of Aaron. Aaron's order is explained absolutely, without question, by our schoolmaster, the Old Testament.

The Order of Aaron

And take thou unto thee Aaron thy brother, and his sons with him, from among the children of Israel, that he may minister unto Me in the priest's office.... And thou shalt make holy garments for Aaron thy brother for glory and for beauty.

Exodus 28:1-2

This passage goes on to say that Aaron must have a breastplate, an ephod, a robe, an embroidered coat, a mitre and a girdle—the garments we discussed in the previous chapter.

And thou shalt put them upon Aaron thy brother, and his sons with him; and shalt anoint them, and consecrate them, and sanctify them, that they may minister unto Me in the priest's office. ... And they shall be upon Aaron, and upon his sons, when they come in unto the tabernacle of the congregation, or when they come near unto the altar to minister in the holy place; that they bear not iniquity, and die: it shall be a statute for ever unto him and his seed after him.

Exodus 28:41,43

And thou shalt take of the blood that is upon the altar, and of the anointing oil, and sprinkle it upon Aaron, and upon his garments, and upon his sons, and upon the garments of his sons with him: and he shall be hallowed, and his garments, and his sons, and his sons' garments with him.

Exodus 29:21

This order of Aaron is found in the New Testament as well.

Paul, an apostle of Jesus Christ by the commandment of God our Saviour, and Lord Jesus Christ, which is our hope; unto Timothy, my own son in the faith: Grace, mercy, and peace, from God our Father and Jesus Christ our Lord.

I Timothy 1:1-2

This charge I commit unto thee, son Timothy, according to the prophecies which went before on thee, that thou by them mightest war a good warfare.

I Timothy 1:18

Paul, an apostle of Jesus Christ by the will of God, according to the promise of life which is in Christ Jesus, to Timothy, my dearly beloved son: Grace, mercy, and peace, from God the Father and Christ Jesus our Lord.

II Timothy 1:1-2

> *Wherefore I put thee in remembrance that thou stir up the gift of God, which is in thee by the putting on of my hands.*
>
> II Timothy 1:6
>
> *Thou therefore, my son, be strong in the grace that is in Christ Jesus.*
>
> II Timothy 2:1
>
> *Paul, a servant of God, and an apostle of Jesus Christ, according to the faith of God's elect, and the acknowledging of the truth which is after godliness; ... To Titus, mine own son after the common faith: Grace, mercy, and peace, from God the Father and the Lord Jesus Christ our Saviour.*
>
> Titus 1:1,4

The apostle Paul had no problem saying to Timothy, "My son, stir up the gift that is in you, which was given you by the laying on of my hands." How could Paul have a son? We do not know that the apostle Paul was ever married. It seems that he did not have a wife. "Have we not power to lead about a sister, a wife, as well as other apostles, and as the brethren of the Lord, and Cephas?"[1] He said, "I am able to lead about a wife as Cephas and the other apostles," but he was unmarried. He had no wife. Yet he called Timothy his son. Timothy was not Paul's incarnate son.

The whole key to the order of Aaron is the priesthood's passing from father to son. There must be a spiritual fulfillment to the type of Aaronic order that passed from father to son. It was in that order and by the laying on of hands and the giving of spiritual impartation that the apostle Paul called these boys his sons. You see, either Paul was very bodacious and had a terrific ego, or there is something very

spiritual and special about the passing of spiritual impartation from a spiritual father to a spiritual son. No one can be
in the ministry unless he has received the impartation from a
father to a son.

Another example of this relationship is Solomon's per-
fecting the house of the Lord in Jerusalem. The vision was
not his own, but that of his father David. For 15 years, while
they were building the temple, Solomon studied the order of
the temple that was written by David. "So the house of the
Lord was perfected."[2] Solomon, "the son," studied the order
of David, "his father." If we do not have a father in the ministry, we have no right to be in the ministry.

No man takes the honor of ministry upon himself. Nobody calls himself to preach. You cannot become a part of
the ministry by yourself. The Scripture says that you must be
called as Aaron.[3] God called Aaron through Moses. Aaron
had no right to the ministry until God spoke to Moses.

Let's look more closely at this concept. In this order, God
first chooses a man. Then He chooses an Aaron. In the Old
Testament, the only way to become a priest was to be the son
of a priest. So we cannot be priests unless we are sons of
priests. In the Aaronic order, it was sonship through physical
generation. Under grace, it is spiritual generation.

We tend to believe that whoever brought us to Christ is
our spiritual father. However, sonship is given when a man
pours his genes (spiritual chromosomes), vision and burden
into another. The man who does that is the other's "father."
The place we can call home is the place where we receive our
spiritual grounding. The Church is our "mother," but we
must have a "father" or we are spiritual "bastards." Where

did you obtain your spiritual direction and guidance? If you can answer that question, then you know who your father is.

Ministry is not the accumulation of academic ability. Ministry is not finally learning enough theology, Christology, epistemology, homiletics or hermeneutics. Ministry is not collecting all those things and saying, "Now I am ready to be a minister of the gospel." You have no right to ministry unless you are called of God, as was Aaron. No man takes this honor to himself. God calls no one to the ministry except men and women who are called of God as Aaron was.

Parameters of the Order

And the holy garments of Aaron shall be his sons' after him, to be anointed therein, and to be consecrated in them. And that son that is priest in his stead shall put them on seven days, when he cometh into the tabernacle of the congregation to minister in the holy place.

Exodus 29:29-30

The priests had to wear their father's clothes or they were not appointed in the priest's office. When it is time for you to be appointed and consecrated to priesthood, you must be in your father's clothes. The son that is a priest in his father's stead shall put on those clothes for seven days. So you must sleep in them and eat in them. You do not take them off for seven days.

And the Lord spake unto Moses, saying, Speak unto Aaron, saying, Whosoever he be of thy seed in their generations that hath any blemish, let him not approach to offer the bread of his God. For whatsoever man he be that hath a blemish, he shall not approach: a blind man, or a lame, or he that hath a flat nose, or any thing superfluous, or a man that is brokenfooted, or brokenhanded, or crookbacked, or a dwarf, or that hath a blemish in his eye, or be scurvy, or scabbed, or hath his stones broken; no man that hath a blemish of the seed of Aaron the priest shall come nigh to offer the offerings of the Lord made by fire: he hath a blemish; he shall not come nigh to offer bread of his God.

Leviticus 21:16-21

So strongly did God make the order of priesthood that, if a son born in the house of a priest had a defect in his body, he could not be a priest. If he had a club foot or a blind eye or if he was ruptured, he could not be a priest. If his stones were broken, if he had a withered hand, or his face was deformed, he could not be a priest. If his nose was pushed to the side or if he had a bad mole or a wart, he could not be a priest. Even if he were born in a priest's house, he had to be without blemish to be a priest.

Also, anyone who was to become a priest had to be so much in love with and so close in association to his father that he would wear his father's clothes when he went to ordination service.

The Father's Impartation

We have not reached the world for Christ because we have put an anemic ministry with a powerful gospel. That has created a vacuum out of the concentration that God intended to be in the ministry. Many ministries do not make a place for their own submission. They are a law unto themselves. Any ministry that becomes a maverick begins a very treacherous course into spiritual perversion. There is no place in the gospel for men to stand alone. We must have one another. If we seek to sever ourselves from our roots in the gospel, we move outside the realm of spiritual ordination.

If there is any tie or cord that should be kept dear and strong, or any landmark that should be polished and kept honored, it should be our relationship with the men of God who laid their hands on us, ordained us, and appointed us to the ministry.

> *For though ye have ten thousand instructors in Christ, yet have ye not many fathers: for in Christ Jesus I have begotten you through the gospel.*
>
> I Corinthians 4:15

You may have many teachers and instructors. You may have been taught by a dozen different professors in the seminary, but you do not have very many fathers. You have no right to ministry if you do not follow the order of Aaron, from father to son.

If no man can take this honor upon himself, then he must have an impartation of honor. Even Christ did not call Himself to preach. Jesus had no right to ministry until God said, "Thou art My Son." Jesus' Father confirmed Jesus' ministry when Jesus was baptized, fulfilling all righteousness. A voice came from Heaven.

> *And Jesus, when He was baptized, went up straightway out of the water: and, lo, the heavens were opened unto Him, and He saw the Spirit of God descending like a dove, and lighting upon Him: and lo a voice from heaven, saying, This is My beloved Son, in whom I am well pleased.*
>
> Matthew 3:16-17

If God had not said to Jesus, "This is My beloved Son," He could not have healed the sick or raised the dead. He would have had no right to ministry.

"No man taketh this honour unto himself." You cannot call yourself to preach. You cannot call yourself into the ministry. You cannot, by private inspiration, determine your calling in God. God gave the order and type in the Old Testament. "And no man taketh this honour unto himself, but he that is called of God, as was Aaron."[4]

"So also Christ glorified not Himself to be made an high priest."[5] Christ did not call Himself to preach. What right does Jesus Christ have to be high priest? What right does Jesus Christ have to be our Mediator? What right does He have to be the Shepherd of the sheep? What right does He have to be our Lord, Preacher and Lawgiver? Who gave Him the right? In talking with the Samaritan woman about the Messiah, Jesus said, "I that speak unto thee am He."[6] Did that give Him the right? He already had the right. When they said, "Are you a king?" He said, "Thou sayest that I am a king. To this end was I born, and for this cause came I into the world."[7] Did that make Him a king? He was already a king.

What made Jesus what He said He was? He said that He was the Messiah. He said that He was the Anointed. He said that He was a king. He said that He was the Lord. He said that He was God in flesh. "Before Abraham was, I am."[8] They said, "You are not even 50 years old, and You say You lived before Abraham?" He said, "Abraham rejoiced to see My day."[9] He acknowledged Himself as being eternal. Did that make Him the priest? What made Him a priest? What gave Him the right to priesthood?

So also Christ glorified not Himself to be made an high priest; but He that said unto Him, Thou art My Son, to day have I begotten Thee.

Hebrews 5:5

Jesus did not call Himself to preach; it was He who said, "Thou art My Son, to day have I begotten Thee." It was the word of the Father, spoken of the Son in the river, that gave Jesus the right to be both the sacrifice and the sacrificer. He had the right to offer Himself as well as to become the offering. He had the right to priesthood only because the Father said, "This is My beloved Son...hear ye Him."[10] The only right that Jesus had to ministry was the fact that He was the Son of the Father. Therefore it was after the order of Aaron.

The Father did it twice, once in glory and once in water; once in spirit and once in water. Jesus stood in water, and the voice from Heaven said, "This is My beloved Son, in whom I am well pleased."[11]

At age 30, the priest was to wash "withal" (or all over) at the brazen laver of water.[12] He washed in oil and in water (water and spirit). He washed in the laver at 30 years of age and entered into the priesthood. Jesus was 30 years old when He entered the priesthood at the hands of John the Baptist. He too entered the ministry by water and spirit.

Jesus stood in the water, a dove descended, and a voice came from Heaven and said, "Thou art My beloved Son, in whom I am well pleased."[13]

On the mount of transfiguration, in glory before Peter, James and John, the same voice said, "This is My beloved Son, in whom I am well pleased; hear ye Him."[14]

Jesus had the right to ministry. So you can believe everything He says. He is a priest. He is Lord. What gave Him the right? The Father said, "He is My Son." The ministry passes from father to son.

Submission to your father in the gospel gives you the right to ministry. That is the only action that will do so.

Credentials will not do it. A license will not do it. Somebody has to say, "He is my son." If a man of God cannot say that about you, and you cannot look back to an experience in which somebody, in his understanding of God, found you worthy to call his son, then you do not have a calling in the ministry.

The Passing of Vision

Men and women who do not have the proper vision still start many churches today. They are splinters of other churches, however, and will never amount to anything. They may gather a group of people together, but they will always be out of the will of God. Even though they may justify themselves, God still calls for repentance. It is God who establishes a man, and God will do the removing and the chastening. We have no right to call ourselves to the ministry, regardless of the circumstances.

The only chance we have to ministry is through our spiritual fathers. That means we must find a spiritual father and, once we have found him, guard his vision. Even then, my spiritual father must be able to say of me, "He is an able man, a God-fearing man, a man of truth who hates covetousness." If he says that of me and lays his hands upon me, then his spirit and his vision become mine.

A little church sits on every corner because someone could not get along with someone else. The Church, which should be a work of unity and of the Holy God, has become the sign of division. Some preachers are sent and others just went.

Men have bred divisiveness, inconsistency and anemia into the ministry. A weak ministry then breeds weak children. Those who come up under those ministers do the same things. Thus we spread sickness and religion that cannot touch cities for Christ.

If you want a great plow horse, you buy a Belgian mare and you breed it to a stud horse. That is how you produce a strong colt. God's intention was to set powerful men and women in the Church to sire able men, honest men, godly men, and men without covetousness.

Preachers are to be righteous and godly men, but by the same token we must recognize that they are also mortal and in need of assistance and consolation at times. After all, when Moses became angry with the people, he broke the tablets of the Ten Commandments. God then made other tablets to replace the ones that were broken. Moses displayed human anger, but he was still God's man. So men and women of God are not without mistakes. We should allow them to be human. On the other hand, even though they have human frailties and faults, we must respect and honor the office God has given them.

Still, if a minister cannot point back to a spiritual father, then he is not a son; he is a "bastard." Someone who is truly called must be able to stand by his spiritual father and guard his vision. "If my spiritual father places me in authority, I will stand with my sword drawn and guard his back," is the son's cry. If authority is given to us, we must not allow any harm to come to our spiritual fathers. We must guard them with our lives. By guarding them, we protect our hope and usefulness in the Kingdom of God.

The Prophets Elijah and Elisha

The relationship between Elijah and Elisha is a powerful example of this spiritual impartation between father and son.

And it came to pass, when they were gone over, that Elijah said unto Elisha, Ask what I shall do for thee, before I be taken away from thee. And Elisha said, I pray thee, let a double portion of thy spirit be upon me. And he said, Thou hast asked a hard thing: nevertheless, if thou see me when I am taken from thee, it shall be so unto thee; but if not, it shall not be so. And it came to pass, as they still went on, and talked, that, behold, there appeared a chariot of fire, and horses of fire, and parted them both asunder; and Elijah went up by a whirlwind into heaven. And Elisha saw it, and he cried, My father, my father, the chariot of Israel, and the horsemen thereof. And he saw him no more: and he took hold of his own clothes, and rent them in two pieces. He took up also the mantle of Elijah that fell from him, and went back, and stood by the bank of Jordan; and he took the mantle of Elijah that fell from him, and smote the waters, and said, Where is the Lord God of Elijah? and when he also had smitten the waters, they parted hither and thither: and Elisha went over. And when the sons of the prophets which were to view at Jericho saw him, they said, The spirit of Elijah doth rest on Elisha. And they came to meet him, and bowed themselves to the ground before him.

II Kings 2:9-15

Elijah saw Elisha in the field, placed his own mantle on Elisha's shoulder, and said, in effect, "Follow me."[15] Jesus told the men in the boat the same thing: "Follow Me."[16] There is a spiritual operation that caused these men to obey. There was a choosing. God commanded Moses to bring only those men to the tabernacle whom he knew to be elders.[17] He had to know who were elders. They had to be men who had been compassed with infirmity. They would have to offer sacrifices for themselves. They had been proven by experience to be elders. Sometimes even the man who has been reproached is an elder. Such men have lived and made it through the experience.

Elisha had 12 yoke of oxen and a plow. He was a successful and prosperous young farmer. Yet he left it all behind because Elijah threw a mantle on him. Thus there must be a mantle passing.

Elisha broke up all his plow handles. He killed his oxen and had a big feast. He left his parents and followed that hoary-haired, old preacher-prophet, Elijah.[18] They left their footprints in the dew. They sat around a campfire in Gibeah, by Bezer, and many other places. They prophesied.

There came a time when the aging prophet said, "I am going away." A little later he said, "I will go to Bethel. I need to pray a little." Elisha said, "I will go with you." Elijah said, "You stay here." Elisha said, "I will go with you."[19] That was Elisha's test. The prophet turned to him and said (this demonstrates the tenacity of the relationship), "If you see me when I go, a double portion of my spirit will be on you."[20] Whose spirit? "My spirit," not God's Spirit.

The original language says, " 'If your eyes see what my eyes see' when I go." One translation says, "If we see eye to eye when we separate." For us that means if we leave because we do not like the minister, we have cut off our right to ministry. If we start another church because we failed to get along with our pastor, we are through. We must see what our father sees when he goes away. Our eyes must see if we still wear his clothes.

Elisha would receive a double portion of the "Elijah spirit." If Elisha saw "eye to eye" with Elijah, he would receive a double portion. Elisha would not only receive what he had already gotten from being with Elijah during his life on earth, but also what Elijah himself had. That is the double portion. We cannot ask for the double portion of our spiritual father's spirit if we do not see "eye to eye" with him.

When Elijah and Elisha went on their way to Jordan, they passed by the sons of the prophets. The sons of the prophets had some spiritual inclination. They asked Elisha, "Do you know that your master shall be taken away today? He is going away."[21] God imparted that knowledge to the sons of the prophets. Did Elisha know that Elijah would be taken away? He certainly did. He was hanging on to Elijah's coattail. Elisha would not let Elijah out of his sight. "I have been with him to prayer. I went with him to look at the world. Now I am going down to the water. I will not lose him. Wherever he goes, that's where I will go."

Elijah took off his mantle and hit the water with it. The waters rolled back to the left and to the right and they went across the river to the other side.[22] When they arrived on the other side, they kept walking. Then Elisha said, "What is coming?" "I do not know what that is." "It is coming closer and closer...here comes a chariot of fire!" The thing they saw was blazing, rolling, smoking and shimmering. The chariot of fire came closer until it separated and divided Elijah from Elisha.[23]

Here comes the chariot of fire! Elijah jumped one way and Elisha jumped the other. The chariot went roaring between them. About that time, a big whirlwind picked up Elijah and carried him into Heaven.

When that young prophet of God watched that bold prophet of God go, he did not say, "Elijah! Elijah!" He did not say,

"O prophet! O prophet!" What did he say in relationship to the separation unto the ministry? "My father, my father, the chariot of Israel, and the horsemen thereof."[24] It was a separation in the proper order of ministry: "My father."

How do you separate from the man of God who called you? It was Elijah who said, "Come follow me." Elisha said, "Where are you going?" Elijah just said, "Come follow me. Come on with me." A man of God beckons to you and says, "Come follow me." Then, sometimes, God by His fiery Holy Spirit will separate you into your own ministry.

> *As they ministered to the Lord, and fasted, the Holy Ghost said, Separate* [to] *Me Barnabas and Saul for the work whereunto I have called them.*
>
> Acts 13:2

The chariot was a type of the Holy Spirit. The Holy Spirit is the only thing that can separate ministry unto ministry. "Separate [to] Me Barnabas and Saul." Who said that? The Holy Ghost said that as the prophets and teachers fasted, prayed and ministered unto the Lord.

Impartation in the New Testament

As mentioned before, Paul also addressed Timothy and Titus as his sons in the gospel.

> *Unto Timothy, my own son in the faith: Grace, mercy, and peace, from God our Father and Jesus Christ our Lord.*[25]
>
> I Timothy 1:2

> *To Titus, mine own son after the common faith: Grace, mercy, and peace, from God the Father and the Lord Jesus Christ our Saviour.*
>
> Titus 1:4

Paul gave Timothy his license to the ministry when he laid his hands on Timothy.[26] We can claim ministry when our ministry father says, "This is my son." Even Jesus could not preach if His Father did not say that to Him. Eldership must be a spiritual impartation.

Wherefore I put thee in remembrance that thou stir up the gift of God, which is in thee by the putting on of my hands.

II Timothy 1:6

Jesus then took the total of redemption and laid it on the hot hearts of 12 men, saying, "Freely ye have received, freely give."[27] After He received the confirmation of the Father, Jesus went from miracle to miracle, victory to victory, and glory to glory because He was properly aligned with order. He obtained the order when He asked John to baptize Him. "For thus it becometh us to fulfill all righteousness."[28] John had to put Jesus under the water and bring Him back up, and God had to speak to Him in order for Him to have a ministry.

Paul said to Timothy, "I laid my hands on you and imparted something to you. You stir it up."

For I long to see you, that I may impart unto you some spiritual gift, to the end ye may be established.

Romans 1:11

Paul told the Romans, "I want to come and be with you that I might impart unto you some spiritual thing, in order that you might find out what our relationship is. I am your father and you are my children. The only way the gospel will be spread in Rome is if I can come and impart something to you so you will understand that relationship. If you do not understand that, Rome will be a lusty sinner."[29]

When God raises up a man in a city, it is natural for him to have children, or followers. We still may try to separate ourselves that we may be exalted, but the only way our own ministry can be exalted is for us to submit one to another in proper relationship, in the fear of God.

Also, there is no unity without submission. If we do not pour the anointing oil on the head of our leadership, then the anointing cannot flow down to the hem of the garment. How can we be anointed around the knee area if we are not willing to anoint the head? Anointing flows down from the top. In order for God to establish us, we must be willing to work under spiritual authority.

Wait Until the Time Is Right

After Elijah was gone and they needed a man to be the prophet of God over them, the sons of the prophets said, "Who will take Elijah's place?"[30] The king of Israel, the king of Judah, and the king of Edom were gathered together. They said, "Who will speak the word of the Lord to us?" The king of Moab had rebelled against Jehoshaphat. The kings wanted to know, "Which way shall we go into battle?" They did not know the best way to go. Still, they went ahead and journeyed through the wilderness of Edom. They fetched a compass and set a seven days' journey. However, there was no water.[31]

Today such leaders come together and say, "What do you think is the best thing for us to do for this church? What do you think we should do? Should we buy this or should we go there?" Like the kings, they say, "Go this way." They go seven days and there is no water. They run out of spirit.

The king of Israel said, "Alas! that the Lord hath called these three kings together, to deliver them into the hand of

Moab!" But Jehoshaphat said, "Is there not here a prophet of the Lord, that we may enquire of the Lord by him?" One of the servants of the king of Israel answered. He grabbed somebody by the sleeve, pulled him out, and said, "Here is Elisha the son of Shaphat, which poured water on the hands of Elijah." Jehoshaphat said, "The word of the Lord is with him."[32]

When it came time for a true word of God, they looked for the young man who had served the old man of God. Where is the young man who poured water on the hands of Elijah? He would be a prophet for them.

> *Now I say, That the heir, as long as he is a child, differeth nothing from a servant, though he be lord of all; but is under tutors and governors until the time appointed of the father.*
>
> Galatians 4:1-2

It is the father who says, "Now." The father says, "You have been my son all this time, but now you have authority to do this thing." You may say, "But I have the knowledge and I know God has called me." You still should not go anywhere until a father says you can go. If you do go beforehand, you are out of order. All of us are under tutors and governors. We learn and study until the father says, "All right. It is time."

> *Even so we, when we were children, were in bondage under the elements of the world: but when the fulness of the time was come, God sent forth His Son, made of a woman, made under the law, to redeem them that were under the law, that we might receive the adoption of sons. And because ye are sons, God hath sent forth the Spirit of His Son into your hearts, crying, Abba, Father.*
>
> Galatians 4:3-6

Elisha cried, "Abba, Father." That is the only right we have to be a son of God.

This right is more than just having the legal right to preach on the street. It is more than a certificate that says, "You have joined the elite crowd of preachers in this world." If we find God's pure line of impartation, we will understand why the apostle Paul would make this statement:

"I want to be with you. I need to see you because I want to impart unto you some spiritual gift, in order that you may be established. I want to be comforted together with you. I want my mind straightened out. I want to be sure of you by the mutual faith of both you and me. We need to have the proper relationship. That is the only way Rome will receive the gospel. We must know where we are and be comforted in our relationship together."[33]

End Notes

1. I Corinthians 9:5.

2. II Chronicles 8:16c.

3. Hebrews 5:4.

4. Hebrews 5:4.

5. Hebrews 5:5a.

6. John 4:25-26.

7. John 18:37.

8. John 8:58.

9. John 8:56-57.

10. Matthew 17:5.

11. Matthew 3:17.

12. See Exodus 40:30, Leviticus 8:6 and I Chronicles 23:3.

13. Mark 1:9-11.

14. Matthew 17:1-8.

15. I Kings 19:19.

16. Matthew 4:18-19.

17. Numbers 11:16.

18. I Kings 19:19-21.

19. II Kings 2:2.

20. II Kings 2:9-10.

21. II Kings 2:3,5.

22. II Kings 2:8.

23. II Kings 2:11.

24. II Kings 2:12a.

25. See also I Timothy 1:18 and II Timothy 1:2.

26. See I Timothy 4:14 and II Timothy 1:6.
27. Matthew 10:8.
28. Matthew 3:15.
29. Romans 1:11-13.
30. II Kings 2:15.
31. II Kings 3:5-9.
32. II Kings 3:10-12.
33. Romans 1:11-13.

Chapter 5

The Anointing and Sacrifice

In the anointing, the holy God of Heaven becomes aligned with our spirits so we humanly manifest the deity of God. When you sing, it is not your song but His song. When you preach, it is not your sermon but His word. When you witness, it is not your experience, but God's life manifested through you. The anointing is the very essence of God.

> *No man hath seen God at any time; the only begotten Son, which is in the bosom of the Father, He hath declared Him.*
>
> John 1:18

We cannot look at Him. Two milleniums have not erased the glory of His earthly presence. Have you ever wished you could see Him? You must see Him through His Word. You must hear Him in a son. You must hear Him in a message. You must love Him in somebody's praise. One day, we will see Him as He is in all His glory. Now, we must live for the anointing.

Expressing the Anointing

The Old Testament priests were the first to express the anointing. Then the prophets expressed it. They used the oil, which was a type of the Spirit, to express the anointing.

For special events, or when someone was to be used in a special way, a ram's horn held the oil.

One of the first things described in the Old Testament covenant was the preparation of the anointing oil. Olives were beaten. Then they were mixed in with a special formula (which we discussed previously) to form the oil. It had to have a fragrance and an essence. The eyes had to see it. The nostrils had to smell it. The hands could touch it. It was the expression of what would later come to the Church in Jesus Christ. Jesus anoints us with the glory and the gladness of His presence. Thus the essence of Christ is in His Body.

God used the anointing to set apart the prophet. The prophets had to have the essence of God to reign and to see. Otherwise, they could see only as far as mortal eyes could see. They could direct only as far as minds of men can direct without the anointing. With divine direction, the prophet prophesies as one who speaks the sight of God. Even our songs contain things angels wish to do that we can do because we have the essence.

The Prophet Samuel

Samuel is one of the most well-known prophets of the Old Testament. He was taken from his mother when he was a very small boy. His mother had taken him to church and handed him over to Eli, the high priest. She had promised in that very place to lend her son to the Lord if God would only give her a son to lend. She promised to lend him to the Lord as long as Samuel lived.[1]

Eli, the high priest, had marked her face that night in the temple. He had slapped her in the face and left a mark. He was chastising her for being drunk in the church. Only, she was not drunk. She had poured out her soul unto the Lord. Then Eli said, "The God of Israel grant thee thy petition."[2]

Samuel's mother did not *give* Samuel to the Lord. She *lent* him to the Lord. She kept the part to pray for him. She kept those rights. A mother whose prayer can open a barren womb is worthy to pray for a lonely boy lying in the back of the church. She may have been praying for him when he first heard the Lord call his name.

And the child Samuel ministered unto the Lord before Eli. And the word of the Lord was precious in those days; there was no open vision. And it came to pass at that time, when Eli was laid down in his place, and his eyes began to wax dim, that he could not see; and ere the lamp of God went out in the temple of the Lord, where the ark of God was, and Samuel was laid down to sleep; that the Lord called Samuel: and he answered, Here am I. And he ran unto Eli, and said, Here am I; for thou calledst me. And he said, I called not; lie down again. And he went and lay down. And the Lord called yet again, Samuel. And Samuel arose and went to Eli, and said, Here am I; for thou didst call me. And he answered, I called not, my son; lie down again. Now Samuel did not yet know the Lord, neither was the word of the Lord yet revealed unto him. And the Lord called Samuel again the third time. And he arose and went to Eli, and said, Here am I; for thou didst call me. And Eli perceived that the Lord had called the child. Therefore Eli said unto Samuel, Go, lie down: and it shall be, if He call thee, that thou shalt say, Speak, Lord; for Thy servant heareth. So Samuel went and lay down in his place.

I Samuel 3:1-9

Thus the Lord raised up a mighty prophet—not one word that Samuel spoke ever fell to the ground.[3] Everything that he ever said came to pass. That is why the men in Bethlehem trembled when that old man came with his perspiration-polished staff and his deep hoary eyes. His word was God's word. Whatever he said was what God said.

And the Lord said unto Samuel, How long wilt thou mourn for Saul, seeing I have rejected him from reigning over Israel? fill thine horn with oil, and go, I will send thee to Jesse the Bethlehemite: for I have provided Me a king among his sons. And Samuel said, How can I go? if Saul hear it, he will kill me. And the Lord said, Take an heifer with thee, and say, I am come to sacrifice to the Lord. And call Jesse to the sacrifice, and I will shew thee what thou shalt do: and thou shalt anoint unto Me him whom I name unto thee. And Samuel did that which the Lord spake, and came to Bethlehem. And the elders of the town trembled at his coming, and said, comest thou peaceably? And he said, Peaceably: I am come to sacrifice unto the Lord: sanctify yourselves, and come with me to the sacrifice. And he sanctified Jesse and his sons, and called them to the sacrifice. And it came to pass, when they were come, that he looked on Eliab, and said, Surely the Lord's anointed is before Him. But the Lord said unto Samuel, Look not on his countenance, or on the height of his stature; because I have refused him: for the Lord seeth not as man seeth; for man looketh on the outward appearance, but the Lord looketh on the heart. Then Jesse called Abinadab, and made him pass before Samuel. And he said, Neither hath the Lord chosen this. Then Jesse made Shammah to pass by. And he said, Neither hath the Lord chosen this. Again, Jesse made seven of his sons to pass before Samuel. And Samuel said unto Jesse, The Lord hath not chosen these. And Samuel said unto Jesse, Are here all thy children? And he said, There remaineth yet the youngest, and, behold, he keepeth the sheep. And Samuel said unto Jesse, Send and fetch him: for we will not sit down till he come hither. And he sent, and brought him in. Now he was ruddy, and withal of a beautiful countenance, and goodly to look to. And the Lord said, Arise, anoint him: for this is he. Then Samuel took the horn of oil, and anointed him in the midst of his brethren: and the Spirit of the Lord came upon David from that day forward. So Samuel rose up, and went to Ramah.

I Samuel 16:1-13

The only time Samuel ever tried to circumvent the word of God was when he was sent to anoint a king. Samuel did everything God told him to do, without question, until he had to anoint another king. God told Samuel to stop mourning over Saul.

Samuel still remembered the tall kid that they had to drag out from under the chariot wheel. He was a humble child from Kish's house. The people shouted, "God save the king!"[4] God did His best to save that king, but Saul would not let God save him. He went downhill from that moment. Saul had a humble beginning, but in the end he wanted to be both priest and king. He invaded the holy things of God.[5] He did not have any patience for God or for the man of God.

Samuel's tender heart was still bleating for the boy he had first anointed. Then God told him not to grieve over Saul anymore. God had found another boy. God told him to take his horn, fill it with oil, and anoint another king.

The very essence of deity was upon him, but Samuel said he could not do it. He said Saul would kill him. Why was Samuel afraid of Saul? None of Samuel's words fell to the ground.

Samuel could speak one word and Saul would die. However, time and peer pressure sometimes make us all tremble. So God made a way for Samuel. He could take a heifer, a young cow. All he had to say to escape the wrath of Saul was, "Come with me to the sacrifice."

Did God have to create a ruse just to get past one man? God put 150 billion galaxies into proper orbit in space. The sun is in exactly the right place to give us heat and not to burn us up. It's 93 million miles away, just the right distance to be helpful and not harmful. God can make a green tree grow out of black soil. He can make a black and white cow give yellow butter and white milk by eating green grass. God fashions the face of a child with His own fingers. Does God have to lie to circumvent a crooked king?

Samuel knew he was going to Bethlehem to anoint a king. God told him to say that he was going to sacrifice. Anointing is power and God. Sacrifice is bloody death and weakness. Sacrifice was given originally because men could not reach God. Sacrifice and the shedding of blood was an acceptable way for men to draw closer to God. Yet why should the Almighty God have to avoid Saul?

> *Then said Jesus unto His disciples, If any man will come after Me, let him deny himself, and take up his cross, and follow Me.*
>
> Matthew 16:24

Samuel discovered that a sacrifice came with the oil. Everybody loves the anointing. Still, it is more than speed and spit. The essence of God is a precious thing. Many have touched the anointing a time or two, but blessed is he who lives in prayer often enough and long enough to roll back the sky far enough to live with the essence of His power continually.

The Sacrifice of the Anointing

David stood beside his jealous brothers with the oil on his head. Just imagine the scene. He had been in the back of the pasture keeping his father's sheep, playing his harp and writing songs, when Eliab came to get him. Eliab was not happy about having to retrieve David. David's brothers lined up and the old prophet poured the oil on David's head...and David was only a child!

It was 15 years before David would know what exactly had happened that day. He lost Jonathan, his precious friend.[6] He hid from Saul in the cave of Adullam.[7] He saw his cities burned with fire and his wives taken from him.[8] He pretended to be a madman so the Philistines would not recognize him as the mighty David who had removed the head of Goliath.[9] He had the essence of God, but he was also called to the sacrifice. He had to put his heart and his shoulder to the task.

David's son was to be a Messiah who would sit on the throne of his father David forever. In his youth, David was running from Saul. In his old age, he was gathering material for a temple that he would not be able to build. This man saw Christ in all His glory, from His birth to His death and to His resurrection.

I have set the Lord always before me: because He is at my right hand, I shall not be moved. Therefore my heart is glad, and my glory rejoiceth: my flesh also shall rest in hope. For Thou wilt not leave my soul in hell; neither wilt Thou suffer Thine Holy One to see corruption.

Psalm 16:8-10

This foundational prophecy from David's pen is the message that started the New Testament church. Nevertheless, God denied him the right to build the temple.

Now it was in the heart of David my father to build an house for the name of the Lord God of Israel. But the Lord said to David my father, Forasmuch as it was in thine heart to build an house for My name, thou didst well in that it was in thine heart: notwithstanding thou shalt not build the house; but thy son which shall come forth out of thy loins, he shall build the house for My name.

II Chronicles 6:7-9

Loneliness goes with the anointing as well. Was David doing the will of God when he cut off his enemies' heads? Was he doing the will of God when he conquered all of Israel's enemies? Did he do the will of God? He paid dearly for doing God's will. David did not just receive the anointing; he also slew the heifer and made the sacrifice.

There must be a sacrifice with the anointing and with great glory. You must carry the cross daily. If you cannot bear the cross, you cannot wear the crown. If you anoint a boy who will be a man after God's own heart, you must take a heifer to sacrifice. In order for there to be anointing, there must be sacrifice.

End Notes

1. I Samuel 1:24-28.
2. I Samuel 1:10-17.
3. I Samuel 3:19.
4. I Samuel 10:17-24.
5. I Samuel 13:9.
6. I Samuel 20:41-42.
7. I Samuel 22:1.
8. I Samuel 30:1-3.
9. I Samuel 21:13.

Chapter 6

Strange Spiritual Children

Blessed be the Lord my strength, which teacheth my hands to war, and my fingers to fight: my goodness, and my fortress; my high tower, and my deliverer; my shield, and He in whom I trust; who subdueth my people under me...Bow Thy heavens, O Lord, and come down: touch the mountains, and they shall smoke. Cast forth lightning, and scatter them: shoot out Thine arrows, and destroy them. Send Thine hand from above; rid me, and deliver me out of great waters, from the hand of strange children; whose mouth speaketh vanity, and their right hand is a right hand of falsehood...Rid me, and deliver me from the hand of strange children, whose mouth speaketh vanity, and their right hand is a right hand of falsehood: that our sons may be as plants grown up in their youth; that our daughters may be as corner stones, polished after the similitude of a palace: that our garners may be full, affording all manner of store: that our sheep may bring forth thousands and ten thousands in our streets: that our oxen may be strong to labour; that there be no breaking in, nor going out; that there be no complaining in our streets. Happy is that people, that is in such a case: yea, happy is that people, whose God is the Lord.

Psalm 144

Many times, when we ask God to anoint us to do something great, mighty and awesome, God manifests things in our lives that cause that power to be restrained. We pray, "God, anoint me! Do a mighty thing through me!" In order for Him to do that thing, however, the Lord must reveal to us things in our lives that we must adjust. I believe that is the point this passage of Scripture makes.

"Great waters" speaks of confusion or a multiplicity of detail. When the waters were upon the face of the deep, things were devastated. Waters can also speak of multitudes. In this psalm, "great waters" is an expression of great consternation or trouble. The Psalmist wants the Lord to deliver him out of great trouble, out of great waters, as well as from the hand of strange children, whose mouths speak vanity and whose right hand is the right hand of falsehood.

The word *strange* precedes the word *children*. Combining these two concepts creates the knowledge of a circumstance that we will compare spiritually to this prayer of David. Strange children. If he had said, "Deliver me from children," we would understand that he was praying he would not have any children. But when he said, "Deliver me from strange children," he qualified the progeny and made it an exclusive group: only those children who were not familiar or who were not righteously the same as he.

Children From Love

Lo, children are an heritage of the Lord: and the fruit of the womb is his reward. As arrows are in the hand of a mighty man; so are children of the youth. Happy is the man that hath his quiver full of them: they shall not be ashamed, but they shall speak with the enemies in the gate.

Psalm 127:3-5

Children are the heritage of the Lord. They are like arrows in a quiver. A man is blessed if he has his quiver full of them. A blessing is pronounced on large families with many children. We, however, live in an age where marriage and family relationships often include birth control to prevent the birth of children. Our society is even busy trying to teach other societies these same methods to stop them from having so many children.

The world was sweeter, better and more wholesome when mothers and fathers had all the children they could. In this age, cats, dogs and cars take precedence over the rearing of our own flesh, life and blood. This trend has brought a curse to our society and a condemnation to our nation.

The love for our offspring should not be given to a cat or a dog. God intended that a human family should bring forth children. In the Hebrew culture, it was a reproach for a woman married in the Hebrew family not to bear children.[1]

And when Rachel saw that she bare Jacob no children, Rachel envied her sister; and said unto Jacob, Give me children, or else I die.

Genesis 30:1

Rachel felt that she could not live if she did not give life to children. What would the world be like without children? Can you imagine a world without children?

I read a story once about a family who adopted a little baby boy. The mother and father originally had made up their minds that they never wanted children. They did not want the responsibility of bringing up a child in the terrible circumstances of the society in which they lived. One day the man was at a store in a market. He patted a little boy on the head and said, "How are you, sonny?" The little boy looked up, and said, "Fine." The little boy then asked, "Sir, where are your little boys?" He said, "I do not have any children. My wife and I do not want any children." The little boy answered him with a question that stunned the man. "Sir, who will look after you when you get old?" When the little boy asked that question, the man went home and told his wife, "We will have children." It was too late in their lives for them to physically bear children, so they adopted a little baby boy to take care of them when they were old.

When love gets in the picture, it destroys all the problems that society has. Children should be the response to, and the result of, love between a husband and wife. Love is the force for producing children. It is not just the act of an affair, of bodies coming together for a chemical or biological purpose working in force with nature to produce children. God intended that Adam love his wife. It is the plan of God that husbands love their wives, that wives love their husbands, and that the response to, and the result of, that love relationship would be children.

Those families who have the proper perspective for having children take responsibility for rearing those children. They perform the sometimes thankless task of providing food, clothing and education (and all that education entails: the textbooks, paper, pencils and pens, rulers and erasers, tennis shoes, blue jeans, little skirts and blouses...).

Children in their younger years are very forthright. One time I met a school child out in the schoolyard on a cold day. He was not wearing his jacket. I said, "Where is your jacket?" He answered, "I do not have it with me. I am out of uniform too." He planned to let me know right away that, if I found fault with his procedure, he would tell me that he knew the rest of his attire was questionable as well. He gave me the whole story at one time. "I am out of uniform too."

The teenage years are a tragic space of time when children grow so wise so quickly. Fathers and mothers lose mentality by the pound, hour by hour, until there is a gigantic generation gap. An enormous chasm in understanding divides adolescents and adults. As parents we try our best to struggle through to their graduation and pray for God to give us grace for college. We hope that somewhere, someday, the love that we have given in misunderstanding and that the lack of purpose in the child's mind will turn into understanding and purpose in his adult heart. That grown child comes back to put a big, rough arm around a withering chin and pull a gray head down upon his breast, and says, "Mama, I love you!" or "Papa, you mean all the world to me." This would be a tragic world without love and lovemaking. What would it be without the production, rearing and maturing of children? That is God's plan.

Without Love

It is possible to have children without love. The body has the ability to produce a child outside the bonds of love. Unfortunately, there is in the mind, spirit, emotions and heart of man a wickedness that is bestial. There is the ability of a man to force his will upon a woman and, without her permission, force seed upon her that she may be with child. We call it rape.

Rape is a terrible word. It has the note of a sword in it. Rapier! Rape! It almost rips the spirit when you say it. If you have been a pastor or have worked in crisis counseling, you know that there is hardly any pain of spirit harder to heal than the pain of a woman forced into a relationship by a thoughtless man.

That is not the only way, though. There is also a sensuous attitude that may find its way into the heart of a maiden that she may wish to sell her body for money. She may wish for some illicit moment of pleasure and look for a back street or a dimly-lit fleabag motel to give herself to someone or something that will make her regret it later. She may try, in the afterglow of an act that should be real and beautiful, to wash her body and her sins in the hope of forgetting that it ever happened. Many maidens, as well as young men, find themselves caught in the trap of an elusive and very tenacious attitude that slips in and weaves itself through the inner cords of their youth. It is lust that takes control of them.

Flee also youthful lusts....

II Timothy 2:22

The natural force of the body creates a chemical change and reaction in the body which in turn creates a mindset that can produce such a wantonness that you eventually desire something or someone even outside the bonds of love. If you let that happen, and you then seek that unlawful relationship, when the affair is over, the deed is done, and you have showered and walked away feeling as if you have cleansed yourself, what a horror it is to learn in a few days and weeks that you carry in your body a lingering of that affair. It was not just a moment's pleasure. Something in that act created an eternal soul.

Today the greatest moral issue in America, and even in the world, is the killing of unborn babies. Abortion has become a political issue. It has become a state, city and welfare issue. It is an issue for preachers. It is an issue for state officials. Abortion is the murder of an unwanted, unborn child. A relationship produces a baby, but partners in that productive relationship never intended for it to be or to grow.

If these children were the product of love, the parents would want them to grow. They are not the product of certain and absolute surrender, however. They are the product of a physical, chemical and biological event.

Strange Spiritual Children

Sometimes people and things induce us to participate in similar mental and spiritual relationships with worldliness. We wander the back streets of unbelief, lie in dark alleys of doubt, or crawl into a fleabag bed with bitterness. When we go back to the foot of the cross and bathe ourselves from that illicit relationship, we allow our minds to think that God does not care. We allow our minds to think the people of God unkind. We let ourselves absorb an attitude that says people do not care about us. We let ourselves get strung out on a spiritual philosophy that says we do not need to be so involved with Christ.

Whatever those illicit, idolatrous thoughts and the relationships they have, we need to bring every thought that exalts itself against the knowledge of God into captivity to the obedience of Christ.[2] If there is one thought travelling in our minds that escapes to have a relationship with doubt, fear or unbelief, we need to go quickly into the recesses of our hearts to capture that wandering spirit and bring it back into submission to the Holy Spirit of God.

Instead, what we usually do is cleanse ourselves in remorse of the deed and say, "I am sorry I felt that way. Lord, forgive me. I never intended to act like that. O God, please put all that under the blood." Sometimes, although we repent for the deed and ask forgiveness for that affair with spiritual ungodliness, we do not realize that we have the seed of a strange child bred into our nature.

That is the reason Christians wonder why they have so much trouble with spirits. Why do Christians always battle demonic forces? What prevents us from rising up in the name of Jesus Christ of Nazareth and casting away these things? It is because we deal with the affair instead of with the seed. We deal with the circumstance and not with the eternity of the affair. We are willing to pray for 15 minutes after the preacher preaches and say, "O God, I do not want that. Jesus, wash me in Your blood and make me clean," not realizing that something is formed in our nature and remains in us.

When a woman has a seed in her body, it forms an embryo. Eyes, nails and bones take form in the womb. Likewise, a formation takes place in our illicit relationships with worldliness and ungodliness. When we allow our mind to travel freely up and down the alleys of ungodliness, it is very likely that a child has formed in us, regardless of how many times we scrub the affair. It is very possible that we may have a child.

David did not pray, "Rid me from strange women." The Bible mentions the word *strange* about 60 times in the Old Testament. Forty of the 60 times (two-thirds of the time), the reference is to "strange gods," "strange women," "strange wives" or "strange fire." Those things are absolutely against God. Two-thirds of the times the Old Testament uses the word *strange,* it refers to things estranged from godliness.

But I see another law in my members, warring against the law of my mind, and bringing me into captivity to the law of sin which is in my members.

Romans 7:23

There is an unearthly struggle in Christendom today. Paul said he could see it even in his own members (his body). The war is the flesh of man against the Spirit of God: the flesh against the Spirit and the Spirit against the flesh. There is a warring and a fighting in man. He said, "I see it in my members. It is in me and I know it."

The Lord also spoke of this spiritual ungodliness through Hosea and the other prophets.

A Look at Hosea

Hear ye this, O priests; and hearken, ye house of Israel; and give ye ear, O house of the king; for judgment is toward you, because ye have been a snare on Mizpah, and a net spread upon Tabor. And the revolters are profound to make slaughter, though I have been a rebuker of them all. I know Ephraim, and Israel is not hid from Me: for now, O Ephraim, thou committest whoredom, and Israel is defiled. They will not frame their doings to turn unto their God.

Hosea 5:1-4a

You are wrong if you think God was speaking only to the nations in this passage of Scripture. God was speaking to Israel and, in spirit, to the Church. Yet people will not stop what they are doing long enough to turn to God.

A curse is in our churches today. We think that we are all right, that we have need of nothing. We obtained God somewhere back down the road and feel as if we do not have to worry about ever needing anything else. Even though we have found Him to be precious and know Him to be gracious, full of mercy and lovingkindness, there is, in man, constant waywardness and continuous war. Thus, without the continuing of the blood in its proficiency for cleansing us, the Church has become full of ungodliness.

We lie to ourselves. We hide in falsehoods. We hide in our music, our singing, our preaching, our church building, and in that many people go to our church. We hide in that we belong to a certain church or that "God saved me 40 years ago." You can hide in any religious idea that you want. It still remains that before God, you stand or fall in the cleansing of the blood. Without the shedding of blood, there is no remission of sin. It does not matter where you came from, what your spiritual pedigree is, who your spiritual father in the Lord was, how many years you have been in the ministry, or how long you have talked in tongues. After you have borne a hundred precious children, you may be carrying a strange child in your body.

They will not frame their doings to turn unto their God: for the spirit of whoredoms is in the midst of them, and they have not known the Lord.

Hosea 5:4

The word *known* in this instance means "to know" as Adam knew his wife. If people do not have a continuous relationship with God, they become spiritually wanton. They cultivate a relationship with the world. Since they do not pray, they sing the "honky tonk" songs and listen to rock on the radio. Since they do not lift up their hearts and their spirits to the Lord God to give Him glory, they find heroes of this world on the football and baseball fields. All over the country people find something to worship. Just because we at one time had an experience with God does not excuse us from having in our spirits the embryo of some strange, worldly, ungodly and distasteful thing.

How will you know if you never call for the cleansing of the blood? How will you know until you are great with that bitterness and it drops something into your arms that you must take care of the rest of your life? I have watched men go to the grave, nurturing bitterness. They rear it, feed it, diaper it, clothe it, educate it and confirm it. They raise those strange, ungodly spirits in their houses, bedrooms, kitchens and around their family tables. In the foyers of churches, they nurture such filthiness, never realizing that the reason they do not praise God and give Him glory is they never stopped in their ode to graciousness long enough to sense that something unclean and filthy was in them. If God does not purge me, I may bear a child that is not clean. (Of course, this is all a spiritual application; I do not mean that we should abort or kill actual babies.)

> *They shall go with their flocks and with their herds to seek the Lord; but they shall not find Him; He hath withdrawn Himself from them.*
>
> Hosea 5:6

Why would you go to church with your flocks and herds? Those were the sacrifices. The people came with their calves and their lambs, their songs and their music, their singing, their special arts, and their instruments. They came with their flocks and their herds—all their worshiping paraphernalia. The Scripture said that when they go to seek the Lord, they shall not find Him. He will withdraw Himself.

> *They have dealt treacherously against the Lord: for they have begotten strange children....*
>
> Hosea 5:7

> *Ephraim is oppressed and broken in judgment....*
>
> Hosea 5:11

What does that oppression mean? Such people who are oppressed fail to know what is right and wrong. The have such a struggle, even though they have liberty to seek the Lord, to find Him, to do what is pleasing in His sight, and to know Him. They think, "What should I do? Where should I go? Can I do these things? Can I do that? Can I be this way or that? What is this troubled water? What are these many waters in which I am caught? Why do I live my life in spiritual misunderstanding? I do not know whether to go or come. I do not know whether I can do this or that." They have become as oppressed as Ephraim.

The devil cannot completely and totally possess the Christian. Devil possession of Christians is impossible. For someone to be possessed of the devil, he must have totally and completely given over his house to satan. Satan becomes the goodman of the house, the one in charge of the house. I do believe, however, that it is possible for Christians to be oppressed, depressed, suppressed and just pressed. The devil can affect what you think, what you do, and where you go. He can have a complete spell on you and get you to follow his trail. If the Christian ever becomes possessed of the devil, he cannot be possessed of Christ. The Lord will not stay in that house as its Lord and be an inhabitant with the devil.

When someone has evil spirits, it means he had, in the womb of his heart, the embryo of some unclean thing because of a relationship he had with worldliness, unbelieving thoughts, or ungodly attitudes. Growing in the spirit of such a Christian is something that will become a strange child.

The Voice of Strange Children

What exactly is a strange child strange to? It is strange to prayer and worship, to loving one another, to feeding the poor, and to loving your neighbor. It is strange to weeping over a lost world, China, India, or places you have not seen. Those things are strange to the strange spirits. When little strange children pop out of the womb into your arms, and you start taking care of them, they will say, "You do not need to do that. There is no need to go to church. You do not need to pray. That preacher is goofy. The music is too loud." It will criticize everything that has anything to do with godliness or the direction of righteousness, for it is a strange child.

Is it possible to be cleansed from such ungodly attitudes? Of course.

> *And be not conformed to this world: but be ye trans-formed by the renewing of your mind....*

Romans 12:2

Do not conform to the world. Do not become like the world. Be transformed. How can you be transformed? You can be transformed by the renewing of your mind.

What shall we say of those who refuse consecration? What shall we say of men and women who hear sermons but who never act to purge their hearts? What shall we say of those who are not renewed in their minds and in their hearts? What shall we say of people who never consecrate their minds, but who let their thoughts run around like wild banshees, never putting a bridle or a halter on their creative thinking?

You could start thinking that somebody does not like you who has never spoken against you. You simply start think-ing, "She does not like me." After awhile you say, "She does not speak to me." Actually she did not even see you. Then you start saying, "I do not like her, either." Do you know what is happening? That fetus is growing. Your spirit is nur-turing something in its womb. Your spirit is feeding it. The blood flow that should be for worship and glory to God goes to bitterness instead. What should be feeding your strength to do the work of God is feeding bitterness. Then the first thing you know, you have your little diapered baby running around after you. For the rest of your life, every time you try to do something for God or to love people, you will never trust anyone.

Have you heard that baby chatter? "I have learned not to trust people." That is the little embryo you nurtured. That is the little fetus you let grow. When it is time to worship the Lord, you say, "Do I have to stand up again?" That is the little brat you have been raising.

"Ephraim is oppressed and broken." Oppression always breaks your judgment. You do not know what to do because you have too many little voices pulling on you, saying, "Feed me. I am hungry. Clothe me. I have no shoes." By the time you finish with all those little spirits pulling on you, you do not know which way to go. Many people stop attending the house of the Lord because of little voices. People stop giving the Lord of their finances because of little voices. They nurtured those children for a long time. They showered off that compromise and said, "I am through with it. I have forgotten all about it. It will not bother me anymore." They did not, however, have a heart operation. They never removed the seed.

We need a spiritual operation. We need God to take those little things that follow us around and choose what is righteous and unrighteous. If we cannot decide which one we want to raise, we need to say, "God, I do not know what I should do, but somewhere oppression is muddling my judgment."

David's prayer in Psalm 144 was not, "O God, forgive me for this terrible spiritual affair I have been through. O God, forgive me for what I have done in my worldly thinking." He said, "I want you to get rid of the kids." "Deliver me from the hand of strange children." That relationship produced something that lives, breathes, and is as real as the spirit.

When we nurture that strange child, it becomes convenient for us to be as strangers to righteousness. People can speak against the Word of God and feel justified. "I know what the Bible says, but I just cannot stand it." "I know what the Bible says, but...." What is that? Where did we ever get the audacity to say, "I know what God says, but I think...." "I know what God says, but I feel...." "I know they said that they forgive me, but I think they still hold it against me. Every time I am around them I feel just...I just feel terrible."

We may rid ourselves of the little affair, but we are still raising a child, a spiritual baby of bondage, a spiritual child of oppression.

Abraham and Sarah

One of the great biblical examples of this concept is in the lives of Abraham and Sarah.

> *Now the Lord had said unto Abram, Get thee out of thy country, and from thy kindred, and from thy father's house, unto a land that I will shew thee: and I will make of thee a great nation, and I will bless thee, and make thy name great; and thou shalt be a blessing.*
>
> Genesis 12:1-2

> *For what saith the scripture? Abraham believed God, and it was counted unto him for righteousness.*
>
> Romans 4:3

God spoke to Abraham and said, "I will give you a son. You will be the father of nations." Abraham will have seed. Abraham will have a child. Yet as the years went by and time moved along, questions arose. Misunderstanding and lack of knowledge entered the situation.

> *Now Sarai Abram's wife bare him no children: and she had an handmaid, an Egyptian, whose name was Hagar. And Sarai said unto Abram, Behold now, the Lord hath restrained me from bearing: I pray thee, go in unto my maid; it may be that I may obtain children by her. And Abram hearkened to the voice of Sarai.*
>
> Genesis 16:1-2

Now, Abraham was not trying to do anything bad. Abraham was not lusting after Hagar. Abraham loved Sarah. Sarah said, "Take my handmaid Hagar and bear a son by her." That was an effort to do the work of God. It was an effort to help God out. Hagar bore a son and they called his name Ishmael.[3] He was a sweet fellow when he was little, but he was a strange child. Abraham loved Ishmael. Abraham circumcised his son Ishmael. Later Sarah saw the son of Hagar, the Egyptian, mocking her own son. Mocking!

If you want to know whether you have a strange child in your house, that is what it does. It talks back to spirituality. It makes fun of worship. It makes light of prayer. It tries to steal and harden mercy. It tries to overcome your spirituality. It tries to outdo and suppress righteousness.

When Sarah saw the Egyptian's boy Ishmael mocking, she told Abraham, "Cast out this bondwoman."[4] When Sarah talked to Hagar the first time, she said, "She is my maid." After Hagar bore that strange child, she became a bondwoman.

When you have a child by another spirit, it becomes a bondservant. That is what worldliness and ungodliness become to you. They are just servants to please you as long as you are having a little spiritual affair. You feel like no one should say anything. "It is my business where I go, what I look at, and what I wear." I want to inform you that when you have an affair with worldly lusts somewhere in that flea-bag motel, and after you get through with your shower at the cross, there may be in your heart the seed of something you cannot so easily dispose of. It may hang on you for years. You may struggle with it all your life.

To this day you can find Hagar's boy perched on the hills of Golan. He is in Syria and Libya. He is a bloodthirsty terrorist. He does not care for human life. After four milleniums, he is still a ruthless cutthroat. He hates God's people.

Sarah knew what had to be done. She said, "Cast out this bondwoman and her son." A little superfluous repentance is not what we need. What the Church needs today is a gut-wrenching, Holy Ghost revival that gets into our spirits and changes our minds and our lives. We have played too many games at Calvary. We have turned the knob of rusty nails and waited for the splashing shower of the blood. If we can scrub our epidermis, we think we are all right. However, the Church needs to search its heart.

Search me, O God, and know my heart: try me, and know my thoughts: and see if there be any wicked way in me....

Psalm 139:23-24

You might get rid of the woman and yet still have the baby. So David said, "Deliver me of strange children."

Choosing Between

The twentieth-century church knows little of pure revival. We still like worldliness. We can qualify so many things in our spirits. "I know I need to get right, but I do not feel too bad about some things."

Abraham loved Ishmael. His heart was broken for Ishmael. He said, "Ishmael is my son." God took care of Ishmael because he was the seed of Abraham.[5] Yet Abraham had spawned, bred and created something that would haunt his race forever.

For it is written, that Abraham had two sons, the one by a bondmaid, the other by a freewoman. But he who was of the bondwoman was born after the flesh; but he of the freewoman was by promise. Which things are an allegory: for these are the two covenants; the one from the mount Sinai, which gendereth to bondage, which is Agar. For this Agar is mount Sinai in Arabia, and answereth to Jerusalem which now is, and is in bondage with her children. But Jerusalem which is above is free, which is the mother of us all.

Galatians 4:22-26

Mount Sinai "gendereth to bondage." Mount Sinai is Hagar. These two mountains, Sinai and Zion (Mount Zion is Jerusalem), are parallel to these two spirits, Hagar and Sarah. The seed of Hagar, the bondwoman, is Sinai. Sinai is the law. It is bondage. It "gendereth to bondage." When it has a child, it will be bondage. That is what "gendereth" means. When it has children, the children will be bondage.

The Jerusalem that is above us, however, is free, and is the mother of us all.

For ye are not come unto the mount that might be touched, and that burned with fire, nor unto blackness, and darkness, and tempest, and the sound of a trumpet, and the voice of words; which voice they that heard intreated that the word should not be spoken to them any more: (for they could not endure that which was commanded, And if so much as a beast touch the mountain, it shall be stoned, or thrust through with a dart: And so terrible was the sight, that Moses said, I exceedingly fear and quake:) but ye are come unto mount Sion, and unto the city of the living God, the heavenly Jerusalem, and to an innumerable company of angels, to the general assembly and church of the firstborn, which are written in heaven, and to God the Judge of all, and to the spirits of just men made perfect, and to Jesus the mediator of the new covenant....

Hebrews 12:18-24

The new Jerusalem spirit does not allow spiritual imperfection. I may always be imperfect in the flesh, but in my spirit, my attitude, my motives, my heart, my mind and my life, there is a Spirit of God that gendereth to liberty. Everything born of it is free, pure, righteous and joyous in the Holy Ghost.

This glorious liberty we have in Christ should take us out of illicit relationships and ungodly affairs. Jesus Christ should become the Lover of the Church. The Church is His wife. The Church should not be a whoring church. The Church should not be playing and dabbling in iniquity. The Church is to be holy, righteous, pure and clean before God.

What a marvelous opportunity we have! We do not need to live with the bondwoman's children all our lives. We can take them to Calvary. It will not be something bad, something that hurts society, for God to pull out of our spirit the fetus of unbelief. We need God to remove from our arms the spirits of these strange, unparticipating children.

There is a new covenant. The grace of God will perform an operation on your heart. It is the operation of God through the spirit. You do not have to raise that strange spiritual child. You do not have to raise that attitude. You can live for God in harmony, peace and happiness. Torture does not have to accompany you every mile of your Christian journey. We have come to the new Jerusalem and to the innumerable company of angels.

Angels watch this operation. They marvel because they cannot understand it. Angels have never felt redemption's glowing touch. Redemption will never come to the angels that fell. In the darkness of their pit, there are no altars. In the horror of their loneliness, there is not bloodshed. They remain chained under everlasting darkness until the judgment of the great day.

Why should we live in great waters and in distress every moment because oppression has broken our judgment and we cannot tell what is right and wrong?

When we say we will fast and refrain from eating, that little spirit says, "I do not have to do that. I do not believe fasting does any good." Where did you get that little child of unbelief? It is the same spirit that says, "It does no good to call the church. Nothing ever happens when you call for prayer. Why not just take some medicine and be done with it?" Who said that the prayer of faith does not heal the sick? I must believe in my mind right now that it does heal in order to be healed. I must believe that the prayer of faith will save the sick and that the Lord will raise them up.[6]

Strange children hide in religious lies. They say that you are all right when you really are not all right. That annihilates judgment in your life. That destroys righteous judgment in your heart.

If we continue to raise that strange child, we will soon not know what is right or wrong. We will not have any line of righteousness because God lays righteousness to the line. God lays judgment to the line and righteousness to the plummet. Let's get rid of these strange children whose mouths speak vanity and who are always lying to us about our soul. They always tell lies about our spiritual condition. They can always find a reason for not worshiping. These little strange children will always tell us that we have no need to be in church, that we do not have to love anybody. Strange children always tell us that the poor do not need us. Strange children tell us things that are not true.

If we can get rid of strange children, our sons will grow up as plants in their youth. Our daughters may be as cornerstones, polished after the similitude of a palace. Our garners may be full, affording all manner of store. Our sheep may bring forth thousands and ten thousands in our streets. Our oxen may be strong to labor that there be no breaking in or going out. Then there may be no complaining in our streets. Happy is that people. Yes, happy is that people whose God is the Lord.[7]

End Notes

1. Genesis 30:23.
2. II Corinthians 10:5.
3. Genesis 16:15.
4. Genesis 21:9-10.
5. Genesis 17:18-20.
6. James 5:15.
7. Psalm 144:12-15.

Chapter 7

The Desire for Revival

When an individual goes to prayer, everything that enters that prayer closet is what makes that person who he is. He does not just take his body in there; he takes his character in there. He takes along his mind and all his problems. He carries his feelings in there as well. When he pours himself out to God, whatever he leaves with is the result of that supplication. Prayer should be a communion relationship, a reciprocal relationship, with God. Some people, however, never seem to leave their prayer closet with anything, for they lack maturity and spiritual character.

You need to work out through prayer whatever is eating you. Otherwise, it will work you out until nothing much is left of you. Work it out in prayer. Prayer is the key to revival. Let me repeat that: Prayer is the key to revival, to great revival. Great prayer brings great revival. Great singing will make you feel good and even make you think. Sometimes great singing also makes you weep and feel great emotion. Great preaching usually reaches great minds, but prayer reaches God. It is God whom you must reach.

A congregation should never foster the spirit of competition. Just because somebody can play an instrument does not mean that she is more spiritual than somebody else who carries his Bible and witnesses during the day, or than a housewife who keeps her children and cares for the home.

Spirituality is the result of prayer, not of church works. You can go to church regularly and not be spiritual. You can sing all the songs. You can sing in the choir or be an usher at the door. You may count the money or help the poor down at the mission, and you can still not be spiritual. It is possible to be a preacher and not be spiritual. It is possible to be a pastor and not be spiritual.

The most explicit illustration of life and of life's lessons is in the Book of Ecclesiastes, where its author addresses timing. There is a time to everything under the sun. There is a time to be born, and a time to die. There is a time to build, and a time to tear down that which is built. There is also a time to plant.[1]

When I started my garden, some people came to help me plant it. I had planned a big garden. Those people were out there making rows with a hoe, then dropping seeds in my garden. It was a time to plant. Later there would come a time when I would need to plow all that under, when the time of the garden's fruitfulness would have passed. So there is a time to pluck up that which is planted. There is a time to gather stones, and there is a time to throw stones away.

Now is the time to do something of which six months from now we will need to do the very opposite. Thus flexibility is important for the Church. If we have flexibility, we can worship here, and then we can bless someone else there. But there is more to flexibility than even that.

Spiritual flexibility is being able to move with the Spirit. When the Spirit moves (when the cloud and the fire moves), we too must be able to move. There is a time to weep and a time to laugh. There is a time to rejoice and a time to be sorrowful. There is a time for everything. A pastor must find that ebbing and flowing tide.

Our moral and spiritual responsibility to God is to bring forth children. It is best for a mother to conceive and bear children when she is strong. When she is young and strong, she can give birth more easily, and the children are born much stronger.

Drill for Spiritual Oil

God gave me a spiritual philosophy years ago when I was seeking Him in fasting and prayer. By the way, the time when you are down on your face in the lowest dungeon is not the time to seek revival. That is not the time to start screaming. If that is the only time you *can* seek revival, then you must do it. But when you rise up to where you can see daylight, then reach for more daylight. When you get a little faith, reach for more faith. When you gain some victory, reach for more victory. We should go from glory to glory. That is how we change into the image of the Lord. That is the only way we will go beyond our position of the past. Otherwise we simply climb down to where we were. Otherwise revival only brings us back to where we used to be. I used to hear every preacher say, "People need to get back to where they used to be with God." I never heard anybody say very much about going beyond to obtain something else from God.

During that time of fasting and praying, when I suddenly realized that there were fields of spiritual petroleum, everybody else seemed to be having an energy crisis. I don't mean just a physical energy crisis, but a spiritual energy crisis.

Pastors today are still crying for help. All over the country they are calling for revival because nothing is happening anywhere. It seems like things are cold and dead. The Church, in general, seems to be in the midst of a low, low tide. It should not satisfy us, however, to simply accept the status quo and join the ranks of the legions who march to a murmuring monotone and a muffled drumbeat when we can march with the blaring of spiritual coronets and keep time with the Holy Ghost of God. We can walk in the light of His faith and love and be baptized with His own glorious Spirit of understanding.

> *Howbeit when He, the Spirit of truth, is come, He will guide you into all truth.*

> John 16:13a

Close beneath us are the magnificent geysers of His power. Why do we not drill down through carnal flesh with its depression and frustration until we find untapped sources of God's glorious revival for the Church? It takes an overwhelming desire.

The Passion for Revival

> *And when Rachel saw that she bare Jacob no children, Rachel envied her sister; and said unto Jacob, Give me children, or else I die.*

> Genesis 30:1

Rachel angered her husband, Jacob. She made him mad. We make a lot of people mad when we pray for revival because revival brings crisis. Crisis is not popular. People do not want to trouble the water when things are going well. But I have lived through too many dead situations. I have preached to too many dead congregations. I have seen too many moss-covered saints who were supposed to be serving

God, but who had evidently lost their desire and enthusiasm many years earlier. Christianity, to them, was a society. Anybody could come to church. That's like any old fish can float downstream, but it takes a live one to go against the current. Everybody falls apart when we have a little struggle because we usually just float with the tide.

If we are to live for God in this last day, we must become tough. If we walk with God in this end time, we must be strong. We cannot make it by going to church and saying, "I will do the best I can." It is not enough to do the best we can. We must do the best God can. It takes the best God can do for us. We cannot make it by ourselves. We need God every day. The housewife needs God. The lady working on the job and the contractor out on his job both need God. The boys and the girls at school need God. We all need the Lord.

We need God more than in the casual or general sense. We need to call on God. In our minds and spirits, we need to be reaching further than we have ever reached for revival. Our minds ought to be focused on revival every day. Every hour, we need to be praying. Preachers can preach night after night with a burden breaking their hearts and people will walk away the same as they have always been.

The prayer meeting is the Cinderella of the modern church. The prayer meeting is the undesirable scrub woman or the tattered garment. There are no beautiful pearls hanging around the neck of an old-fashioned prayer meeting. On the other hand, everybody loves the luster of the polished choir. Anybody can come to church and be moderately entertained by some average preacher.

Preaching is not always spirituality, as I said. Oftentimes, it is a display of talent, of an ability in a man to expostulate in some manner. All it takes for some men to preach is a sense of accomplishment, some verbal talent, and some moderate text of Scripture. They can generalize until your ears fall off in your lap and make you feel like you have been somewhere, but when you walk out the door, you are no stronger than you were when you walked through it. Today there is too much creamy preaching and not nearly enough steel in believers' blood.

We do fine as long as everything goes smoothly. However, crisis is imminent in this nation. Crisis is imminent in the Spirit. We have never been in a day of pressure as we are today. The pressure is in business. The pressure resides in the home. The pressure builds at the store. There is financial pressure, mental pressure, marital pressure, and every other pressure. The smokescreen is up, trying to misdirect us. If we make it, it will be because we set our face like a flint. Jesus had His face set like a flint to go to Jerusalem.[2] The people who walk in the pearly gate of New Jerusalem also will be people who put their eyes on the heavenly things.

> *Set your affection on things above, not on things on the earth.*
>
> Colossians 3:2

It is one thing to have and enjoy the blessings of life, but it is altogether another thing to love this present world.

> *For Demas hath forsaken me, having loved this present world, and is departed unto Thessalonica....*
>
> II Timothy 4:10

> *And they that use this world, as not abusing it: for the fashion of this world passeth away.*
>
> I Corinthians 7:31

The Bible speaks to us about having things in this life. God tells us to use those things, but not to abuse them. It is all right to have a beautiful home, an automobile and lovely things. God is not against our having nice things.

> *Beloved, I wish above all things that thou mayest prosper and be in health, even as thy soul prospereth.*
>
> III John 2

God wants you to prosper and be in health, even as your soul prospers. You should not have to sell everything you own unless the Holy Ghost lays it on your heart to do so. If He does, then you should sell everything. Nevertheless, you should have wealth. You should be able to save. You should be wise. You should give what you can to the work of God. When the Holy Ghost moves, you should sacrifice and give everything you can.

It is also possible for the cares of life and the deceitfulness of riches to smother the Word of God in our lives.[3] Then all the preaching in the world could not swim its way out of our carnality and worldly lusts. We must absolutely divorce ourselves to some degree from the love of this world and from a love for things or we will never find a place where we can seek God for revival.

The Price of Revival

Revival always finds some hitches along the road. When you start praying for revival, you will find out what you love. When God shows you in prayer the things you need to lay aside, the things you need to lay down, and the things you need to pick up, you are faced with major decisions.

Many people want revival, but not many people get one. Many say they need one, but when they get right down to brass tacks, they are not willing to pay the personal price for a revival. Many people could not get a revival if they wanted one because long ago they spent all their spiritual capital on worldliness and ungodly things. They bought up to the eyeballs in worldly lusts, and a revival will cost them something that they do not have. They have nothing left with which to buy revival.

Little two-cent prayers will never bring God from His throne. You will never turn Heaven upside-down to make the street you live on a revival block by praying little ol' two-dollar prayers that went out of style when you received the Holy Ghost. There must be an unction of spirituality that rushes out through your teeth like a mighty gushing river from some untapped source on the inside that will not be silent. Spirituality says, "I want to pray beyond words. I want to go beyond praises." Revival praying gets beyond clichés. There must be some spiritual groaning that cannot be uttered. There you find God in all His glory.

Because the creature itself also shall be delivered from the bondage of corruption into the glorious liberty of the children of God. For we know that the whole creation groaneth and travaileth in pain together until now. And not only they, but ourselves also, which have the firstfruits of the Spirit, even we ourselves groan within ourselves, waiting for the adoption, to wit, the redemption of our body. For we are saved by hope: but hope that is seen is not hope: for what a man seeth, why doth he yet hope for? But if we hope for that we see not, then do we with patience wait for it. Likewise the Spirit also helpeth our infirmities: for we know not what we should pray for as we ought: but the Spirit itself maketh intercession for us with groanings which cannot be uttered.

Romans 8:21-26

A present condition always becomes worse. So no matter how great your position seems to be at present, if you are satisfied to live there, it will worsen. The only time its value increases and becomes greater is if you use it as a launching pad to obtain some greater position in God. People who have not learned that lesson rise up and attain a particular position in the Spirit, only to find themselves collapsing back down to some lesser place.

Thus comes the little "revival" twice a year, where we bring in a special preacher for two or three weeks of preaching. All the ladies bake pies and we all come to church every night for two or three weeks. When it is over, we count the number of people who received the baptism of the Holy Ghost and say we had a great revival. Yet, the saints still sleep as they did before, unshaken and unmoved. They may have a little more enthusiasm, though; they may buy another bus and load up some more children.

There is more to revival than that trivial demonstration. To be blunt, revival goes down to the guts. It falls down between your eyes and works its way down under your ribs until you cannot sleep at night. Revival makes you love the lost souls you have never met. It makes you weep over people to whom you have never spoken. It makes you want to touch God, even though you don't know why. You feel like you will die if you do not do something.

A Deep Desire

People do not have revival because they do no like to experience that uncomfortable feeling. We prefer all those blessings. We love spiritual services. We enjoy good music and love the preaching of faith. We like to feel that if we are sick, the elders can pray for us and we can be healed. Nobody likes to feel that lowly-gut feeling that drags us along on our toes and nose with our belly suspended over hot ashes, saying, "If I do not receive something from God, I will not make it. I must find a place in the Spirit where these mundane parasites fall from me. I want to soar somewhere higher than the sparrow has ever gone. I want to go beyond where the vultures conceive. I want to move in the Spirit where the glory of God shakes my frame until it moves me into a position that God can honor."

Have you ever noticed that the mightiest men of Scripture were born to barren women? Start with Abraham and Sarah and see that the nation whom God would call His own makes an inheritance through Isaac. God promised a man that He would fulfill all His promises through a barren woman, Sarah. He would make this man's seed as the stars of the heavens and the sand of the sea.[3] All that was brought to pass through the barren womb of Sarah.

Rachel was a barren woman too. Leah already had four little laughing youngsters pulling at her skirts. She was the first wife of Jacob. Although Jacob had worked seven years for Laban in order to obtain Rachel as his wife, Laban tricked him and gave him Leah. Jacob had to work another seven years for Rachel.

And Jacob served seven years for Rachel; and they seemed unto him but a few days, for the love he had to her.

Genesis 29:20

Jacob loved Rachel. His love for her was so great that those years were as a few days. Seven long years was just a small amount of time to Jacob to work for Laban, his father-in-law, so he could have Rachel also. He loved Rachel more than he loved Leah, but God opened Leah's womb and she was very fruitful.[5] Leah bore children, and Rachel bore none. When God finally heard the groaning of Rachel, she bore not simply a son, but a Joseph. She did not bare only Joseph, but also a Benjamin, a "son of my right hand." Her children represented the early and latter rain revivals. Her children and her bearing represented the first and latter parts of the church age.

Joseph was the dreamer, the wanderer and the chosen. Then finally, after all the darkness and the loss, came Benjamin, the last great revival. The bearing of Rachel represented those things thousands of years before they would ever come to pass.

Samson, the strongest man who ever lived, was born of a barren woman—Manoah's wife.[6] Later, Samuel was the greatest prophet who ever prophesied. God did not let one word that Samuel spoke fall to the ground.[7] Samuel was born of Hannah, a barren woman.[8] Ruth, the great-grandmother of David, was a Moabitess who worked her way into the bloodline of the Jewish faith, thus giving us the type of the gentile church. Ruth was barren. She finally bare Obed, and Obed bare Jesse, and Jesse bare David.[9] Elisabeth bore John the Baptist, whom Jesus Christ Himself said was the greatest of all men ever born of women.[10] John was the forerunner of the Lord Himself and the greatest evangelist and preacher that the world had ever known before the coming of the Messiah. John the Baptist was born of Elisabeth, a woman who was barren. Our Savior and Lover, the Redeemer of all the world who rose from the dead and gave us all life, was born of a little girl who knew no man.[11] God gave women who had no children a special, enormous blessing and fruitfulness because of their earnest desire.

The church that so much decries the position of barren-ness is the church that will give birth to great revival. "We do not win enough souls. We do not reach enough lost people," is the cry of Rachel. Any mother who can have a child at any time usually cannot support the ones she does have. If God gave some churches an apostolic revival tonight, they would not know what to do with it. It would not last but a week.

We have hidden behind ourselves for so long, trying to make ourselves feel better, that we hardly know what it means to take a good look at strong meat. We love to just sip on milk.[12] We still look for the bottle. Everyone needs to get his teeth into a good, rare T-bone. We need something to shake us up and make our system work.

Our spiritual system needs to go to work in prayer and supplication. How could these barren women give birth to monarchs and nobles? Why did they give birth to men of promise and Messiahs? The earnest desire is always fulfilled when somebody refuses to accept defeat.

Consider Hannah. She had her head against the cold pillar, sobbing until she could not even make herself understood. Eli, the preacher in the temple, came out and marked her mouth. He slapped her on the face and said, "Woman, you should not be drunken in the house of God." She said, "I am not drunken, but I have poured out my soul before the Lord."[13]

Why would Abraham be the father and Sarah the mother of a promised child who would someday inherit the worlds? Why would they raise up the seed from which a Messiah would be born? Why should they be the ones to father faith for all the human family in every generation that should ever live? Even in this day of grace, we must trace our spiritual genealogy right back to Father Abraham and Mother Sarah.

Without Abraham and Sarah, there are no steps to walk in and no faith to live by. We live by the faith of Abraham, our father.

Jesus said unto them, Verily, verily, I say unto you, Before Abraham was, I am.

John 8:58

Therefore it is of faith, that it might be by grace; to the end the promise might be sure to all the seed; not to that only which is of the law, but to that also which is of the faith of Abraham; who is the father of us all.

Romans 4:16

And think not to say within yourselves, We have Abraham to our father: for I say unto you, that God is able of these stones to raise up children unto Abraham.

Matthew 3:9

That was the cry those men gave as an excuse to Jesus. "Abraham is our father."[14] John the Baptist said that God had power to raise up stones and make them the children of Abraham, and the stones would worship God. God has still neither bypassed nor overlooked that patriarchal lineage.

The Bible is one big chain of people going straight back to two people and one dead womb which belonged to a barren woman named Sarah. Why should she be chosen? She was willing to leave the riches of the Mesopotamian valley. She left her home, her relatives, her gods, and her past to follow Abraham.

Was it riches that Abraham and Sarah needed? They were already rich. Was it wealth they wanted? They had already accumulated it. If they were looking for popularity, they were the finest people in the world at that time. Why should they need to search for social status? The spiritual desire in them already had set them apart. They did not look for wealth and riches. They were not looking for popularity. They were not trying to find social standing. They were searching for a city whose Builder and Maker is God. They had their eyes on something more than what this world could offer. That is the reason God could take a 90-year-old barren womb and turn it into a factory to manufacture a nature that would someday rule the world. Thus the Church that recognizes its condition has the possibility for majestic manifestation of the Holy Ghost.

Travailing for Revival

The church that does not care says, "The children will just get in the way." The church that says, "I do not want any squalling babies around my house" will never have revival. For that church, the three weeks of meeting in March and the two weeks in September just pay an evangelist and keep him on the field.

The church must have more than a preaching series. It takes more than just coming to church and looking at each other and singing the same dead songs. We need to look each other in the eye and say, "If I do not have revival, I will die." God cannot overlook that fervency.

> *For though ye have ten thousand instructors in Christ, yet have ye not many fathers: for in Christ Jesus I have begotten you through the gospel.*

> I Corinthians 4:15

The apostle Paul said that he had begotten those people through the Word of God. He did not say that he had just planted the seed. He said that he had begotten them. There is more to bringing people to God than just saying, "We will preach the Word and it will be good if they accept it, but it will be all right if they do not."

Modern science has helped childbearing. Modern science has certainly diminished the pain that mothers have in childbearing. We thank God for that, but modern science has never managed to shorten the number of months of gestation when the mother carries the baby in her own body. Modern science will not be able to do that. Science will not be able to turn childbearing into a three-month procedure. It takes nine months, unless the child is premature and sick. It takes that long because that is God's plan.

The mother Church also bears children in her womb. There is no shortcut to revival. The church that has the baby is the church that carries it in its own body. It takes more than just preaching the Word and saying, "Put the Word out there. If they want it, they will get it." After the seed is planted, the mother carries it in her own body. She will not let it go. She guards that baby. She does not even go out where other people go. She does not do the strenuous things that other people do. She guards her own body because she has more to do than just keep herself alive. She has some seed in her that someday will live.

The church that has a revival does not just preach and sinners automatically walk in the door. The church weeps over that child. Some nights they do not sleep. Sometimes they vomit in the morning. A church that has revival has to become a mother who carries babies.

> *My little children, of whom I travail in birth again until Christ be formed in you.*
>
> Galatians 4:19

Paul means, in this verse, that he carried those babies all the way from conception to birth. The Church likewise must carry babies. You cannot, like an ostrich, lay an egg and then go off and leave it lying in the sand. In that case every hyena in the world could come by and take a bite. Some churches hope to have revival that way, but revival is not born that way and it will not live that way.

Revival gets inside you and becomes a loneliness. Rachel watched Leah and saw possibility through the children of Leah. Rachel envied the laughter of those tender little faces and flashing black eyes. Those little Hebrew kids turned Rachel upside down. She watched Leah's babies bounce around the floor and laugh and learn to talk. Rachel envied Leah. She was jealous of Leah. She finally prostrated herself on her face before Jacob. Rachel did not say, "I sure would like to have children."

Jacob had not been ignoring Rachel. He had been a husband to her. Jacob had placed Rachel in a susceptible position to receive children. Jacob said, "Do you think I am God that I have withheld from you the fruit of your womb? I cannot help what is wrong with you, woman! I have done all that I can do. God has shut up your womb."[15]

I would rather be marooned somewhere on an island and never see another person's face again than to know that all I could do is maintain what we have managed to build. The Kingdom of God is not a place where we arrive. It is never an earthly utopia. To think that is to kill the engine on this mighty thing. Until Jesus comes again, the whole creation groans.[16] Nothing should be groaning louder than the Church.

Never Give Up

Some people are ready to die. Some people "accept death graciously." Others think, "We will die anyway. Why not just give up?" Other people never give up hope. They will **dig** with their fingernails for hours at the bottom of a rock in a caved-in place until the ivory bone shows through their bleeding flesh because they have a sense of driving hope that they will live a few more days or hours. We will not give up if our children are sick. We will not give up if it is something we love enough.

To illustrate, a few years ago a little boy fell into a hole in his back yard that had at one time been a well. It was a very small, narrow hole. He fell almost 30 feet before he lodged and became wedged in that hole. The fire department and the police and everybody else worked feverishly trying to get that boy out of the well. They could hear the little fellow crying and groaning. He was lodged with his hands straight down. The working men feared that if they dug too close to him, the well would cave in on him. They called a meeting of the emergency people in town. They called in specialists from all over the country. All the while the little boy's mother never left the well. She did not go inside the house to lie down or go to sleep for 72 hours. Those men worked for 72 hours, trying to rescue that little boy.

Men pumped oxygen down into that hole so he could breathe. Once in a while they would hear him sob. He was three years old. They could hear him sobbing and crying a little. They shouted at him, trying to get him to answer. They did not know if he was hurt, broken or bleeding. They finally drilled a big hole to the same depth as the little boy in the well and tunneled across. Finally, they broke into the other hole, caught hold of his little legs, and pulled the dirt back. He fell into the arms of the emergency man. When they brought him to the surface, he was alive.

The little boy's mother was there the whole time. She never slept. She never moved. She would not go away from her little boy. She embarrassed the men when she used the bathroom right there within 15 feet of the place where her baby had fallen into the hole. When they brought the boy to the surface of the ground, they laid him in her arms. After several days of convalescence, he was normal and well. When the reporters asked her later how she had felt, she said something like, "I did not think about how I felt. I would not know how to go back and remember. All I know is that I felt."

Let me give you another example. Ten years ago, when I started doing business in a particular place, the lady there heard that we give our Christmas to the Lord. She became outraged. She threw a big fit in front of everybody who was in the store. She told everybody how horrible we were, mistreating our children like that. Recently, when I was doing business there, she started talking about the young people in this age. She said, "There are some boys that come in here from your church." She named two or three of our young men. She said, "They sure are fine young men. They are so upright, quiet, mature and strong." She looked at me and said, "My two granddaughters are wild and rebellious. I wish they would go to your church. The next time they come to town, I will see about having them go to your church."

Ten years ago, she hated us. Now that she has some wayward grandchildren, she loves us. We cannot afford to be less than we are. Too many people that you do not know have been watching too long. One day, at the right time and place, we will bring them to birth if we are willing to carry them long enough.

More Spiritual Hunger

We cannot afford to rush a revival. If we do, it will be a breach birth, and kill the mother and the baby. The birth

118

must come in its own time and in its own way. That does not mean we are not to plan any part of it. Some people think the revival comes all by itself, and we should not worry about it. Revival, however, never comes to those who do not care. It only comes to those who care when they care enough. Even after we care enough, we still must carry it, maintain it, love it, watch for it, and nurture it until it comes to birth.

What happens to people who do not care about anything? No amount of preaching in the world would change their minds. No amount of crying would change their minds. So God has a little replacement plan He uses. It hurts me to see anybody lose out or go away, but I discovered years ago that God has other people who need that soil and who are willing to live in that sunshine. If you are not willing to grow in God's vineyard and bear fruit, then He has other vines to plant.

"Give me children." It was a ridiculous request. "Give me children." Everything that could be done for Rachel to have children was done. Jacob was not at fault. Rachel was barren. Why did she finally receive a Joseph? Why did she finally bear a Benjamin? Did she bear them because Jacob changed his ways? She received them because she wanted them more than anything else. Read through all the genealogies of the Bible. Did you ever wonder why there are so many "begats" in the Bible? Is that the part of the Bible you skip? Is that part of the Bible unimportant? They don't just fill up space. I read them because they are extremely important. They are the constant reminder of God's intention for the Church. Every one of us should be able to trace his genealogy somewhere. Somebody should be able to trace his genealogy, his spiritual genealogy, back to you.

The stories of these barren women, Sarah and Elisabeth, the wife of Manoah, as well as Ruth and Hannah, have a spiritual application for the Church. If all we do is preach, we will never have much revival. If we had twice as much prayer, we could get by with much less class. If we had a little more travail, we could have less spiritual entertainment. We need a little more spiritual hunger.

Give me children or I will be mad? Give me children or I will quit speaking to you? Give me children or I will go to another church? No. Give me children or my life is over. Give me revival or I will not breathe anymore. Give me a revival or I will not open these eyes in the morning. I will not put food in my belly. I will sing no song and say no poem. I will hold no hand. I will nurture no smile. I will not just passionately change my emotional status, put up my nose, and drop down my mouth. I either have a revival or I die. That is the desire that touches God. Nothing short of that will touch the heart of God.

How much do you want a revival? You probably do not want any more than you know you need. Ninety percent of the people do not feel they need one, for after all, they feel spiritual. They feel God when He moves. They feel the presence of the Lord when they sing. They hear the preacher when he preaches. But we are the ones who need help. We need help in our heads. We need to start thinking, "I must have God."

Revival Is Progressive

When I am near my childhood home in the old Hawkin Valley in central Ohio, I can fill my eyes with fresh memories of yesterday. I can see the autumn trees ablaze with color and the river running low. I am always impressed to remember when they changed the course of the highway. Every visitor I would take through that area would hear me say, "There is where the old road used to be. We used to drive around that way. Then we went over there where that house is built. The highway used to go right through there. There is an old covered bridge right down there and around that bend. We are right where the road used to be, and then it goes off that way. See that little bit of pavement right over there? Then it drops off into a plowed corn field. Through there is where the road used to go."

You can always point out where things used to be because you used to walk there. In my lifetime, I watched that road change three times. The last time it changed, it went through the old cemetery. I used to run through that cemetery when I was a child. All the stories scared me to death. Now the highway goes through it. I have to drive through that cemetery if I go to the town of Logan.

The spiritual commodities around us have increased. So just maintaining ourselves is like keeping up an old country road from 1930. It is narrow, bumpy, and the bridge is out. God's people, however, roll on a superhighway. So we cannot afford to stay where we have always been.

Revival is more progressive than man's mind because it matches God's heartbeat. Just a river did not satisfy God. He made a lake. He was not satisfied with a great lake. So He made an ocean. God was not satisfied with the lonely prairie. He made a hill. It was a good hill, but He made a mountain. He did not only make a mountain, but He made a tall, tall mountain. God is so versatile, He did not only make a world, but worlds of worlds. God did not make just a sun with some planets to go around it. He made galaxies. He made 150 billion of them, and more.

God made so many things that cannot be found even with telescopes, things as big around as 16 and a half feet. They can be seen only as illumination beyond some dark places. Scientists have observed that somewhere on the outer fringes of the darkness, there is an exploding light that goes on and on. When they scan it again, there seems to be a flare where there was nothing. Is it possible that God is so progressive and major that things are still creating as far as the sound of His voice is going? He is still booming out worlds and galaxies and stars and echoing off lunar planetary beings? What a mighty God He is who would progress all the way from innocence to conscience, from a rule of patriarch and human government into a law of religion into a graciousness that has caught us up today. What kind of God would love so much that He would robe Himself in our own likeness, which after He had made in His own, die for us, be buried, rise again, and promise us a world that we have never seen and a hope that we have only felt? What a progressive God to have such a nonprogressive Body.

End Notes

1. Ecclesiastes 3:1-8.
2. Luke 9:51.
3. Mark 4:19.
4. Genesis 22:17.
5. Genesis 29:30-31.
6. Judges 13:2.
7. I Samuel 3:19.
8. I Samuel 1:2.
9. Ruth 4:13,17.
10. Matthew 11:11.
11. Luke 1:34.
12. I Corinthians 3:1-2.
13. I Samuel 1:12-16.
14. John 8:39.
15. Genesis 30:2.
16. Romans 8:22.

Chapter 8

Shall We Weep?

When I was young, we used to have church plays. Everyone would be so excited at Christmastime because we would have a play about the Christmas story. Nothing, however, could match the glory of the Christmas play we had when I was in the junior class at church.

First, we took some sheets and pinned them together with big diaper pins. Those were our curtains. Then we stretched a wire from one side of the building to the other and hooked the sheets on the wire. All the juniors and primary students pulled on the curtains because they could not learn their parts. The only thing they could do was pull the curtains, and they even had problems doing that.

Then the big night finally came. It was announced beforehand and everybody was there. All 52 or 53 church members were sitting in the pews, ready for the Christmas program. The players also had some songs to sing before the program began. They played the music on an old, upright piano with half the ivories missing. The ivories were not all that was missing from that piano. You could hit some of those keys and it played "Silent Night." Nothing came out of that piano when you hit some of those keys.

We had sung our songs and were ready for the curtains to open. The lights were dimmed and there was a sound behind us, but nothing happened. The curtains had been ripped. One side started going back, but the teacher's hand came out, took the curtain, and pulled it back.

Then a little blond-haired girl who played a Jewish Mary came across the "stage." I have no idea, however, what they did to her older sister's clothes to make her look like she had been in the street all her life. Then Joseph came out with his arm around a cardboard donkey, dragging it.

We made those donkeys. We went to Sears where they unloaded the refrigerators. The people who worked at Sears took the refrigerators out of the cardboard crates and put the crates at the back of the store. If we made it to the store before everybody else, we could get those cartons for nothing. So we got them and drew donkeys, camels and sheep on them. We dragged them back and forth across the platform.

The closing of the service is always the best, though. That feeling came to me because of the way we closed those Christmas programs. The pastor always gave every one of the children a big handful of candy or an orange or tangerine. That was the afterglow. We went away saying, "The Lord is in this place." We felt superbly blessed. We loved the close of the service. It was the most spiritual time of all.

Anecdotes aside, there is a part of the Christmas story that is never in the play, and that is fortunate. We do not tell the part that the Scriptures described as happening a few months, perhaps a year and a half, after Jesus was born.

The Sorrowing at Ramah

First came the shepherds. They saw brilliant light and heard angelic voices. The shepherds heard that glorious heavenly host in annunciation, saying, "Go to Bethlehem. You will find there a child wrapped in swaddling clothes, lying in a manger." The Bible said that "they came with haste, and found Mary, and Joseph, and the babe lying in a manger."[1] Then the wise men came from the East, having seen His star, to worship Him. They brought frankincense, myrrh and gold, gifts to give Him. Those stories are full of joy. But there is a part that is not joyous.

> *Then Herod, when he saw that he was mocked of the wise men, was exceeding wroth, and sent forth, and slew all the children that were in Bethlehem, and in all the coasts thereof, from two years old and under, according to the time which he had diligently enquired of the wise men. Then was fulfilled that which was spoken by Jeremy the prophet, saying, In Rama was there a voice heard, lamentation, and weeping, and great mourning, Rachel weeping for her children, and would not be comforted, because they are not.*
>
> Matthew 2:16-18

Herod, the Jewish king, the king of the province, the rebuilder of the temple, the proud and arrogant, selfish and carnal patriarch of Judea, also heard from the wise men about this newborn king. Herod heard that someone was born who would fulfill the prophets' tenure. He would be the fulfillment of what the prophets saw and spoke in prophecy. From his heritage, Herod was acquainted enough with Scripture that he knew this newborn king would be King of all kings. This King would indeed sit upon the throne of His father, David. The renewing of the promise to David of the everlasting Kingdom would belong to this baby, born somewhere in Bethlehem.

Herod was in a frenzy. He said to the wise men, "Go find this child, and when you find Him, bring me news." Herod's devilish lying spirit said, "I will worship Him if you just point Him out to me."[2] The world still tells the same lie. They actually mean, "If you point out the Christ, we will see if we cannot emulsify Him. We will see if we cannot neutralize the Spirit-filled heart. We will see if we cannot destroy the promise."

Messiah was born. That should have forever been a rejoicing for the shepherds. That should have been the song sung not only by wise men, but by all who seek Christ always. To put this portion of Scripture into the joyous coming of Messiah almost destroys the whole feeling of His being. The prophets spoke of Messiah, and said, "Then shall the lame man leap as an hart, and the tongue of the dumb sing: for in the wilderness shall waters break out, and streams in the desert."[3] Eyes will open. Tongues that cannot talk will speak. Deaf ears will hear. The lame people will be able to walk. These were prophecies of great joy. Yet with His coming also came sorrow.

All of Israel had prayed for Messiah. The old men with their caps and their curls would lean their faces against the foundation stones of Solomon's temple. Beneath the shade and shadow of Herod's new structure, they would weep for Messiah.

I asked a person acquainted with the Jewish heart what the most familiar words heard in a temple were. "Hallelujah?" "Praise the Lord?" It is "Messiah."

In the hearts of the Jewish people at the time Jesus was born (most particularly at that time) was the prayer for Messiah. Roman domination and tax collection thrived on every corner. A tax collector sat here and the Roman whip stood over there. The reason Joseph and Mary were even in Bethlehem was a commandment to go back to the house of their fathers for taxation and registration.[4]

That worldwide pressure affected no one more than it did the Jewish nation. They hated the chafe of the Roman whips. They wanted to be free. They prayed for Messiah to come. The young maidens danced in loneliness and cried, "Messiah is coming." The young men warred among themselves and hoped for days when they would serve not the armies of the Romans, but their own army, to liberate their nation. This oppression was too much for the Jewish nation. They prayed for Messiah.

Even the Samaritans who were castoffs from the Hebrew people looked for the coming of the Messiah. When Jesus met a Samaritan woman at a well, she said, "We know that Messiah shall come."[5] It was in their mentality that Messiah would come. All the prophets spoke of Messiah's coming. All the patriarchs prayed for Messiah. Even Caiaphas, Annas and the high priests, from time to time, must have wept for Messiah's coming. However, Messiah stood among them and they did not even know who He was. Herod knew He was there. He ordered soldiers to destroy those children. He had determined to kill the royal seed.

The Wickedness of Herod

Josephus (A.D. 37-100) the ancient historian, was most prolific during the time of the destruction of Jerusalem when Titus and the Roman armies and Vespasian destroyed the city in A.D. 70. He wrote about the antiquities and the histories of the Jews and the wars of the Jews. He recorded how Herod did this terrible thing.

Herod played on the ego of the poor of Judea. He called for a great feast, lining his tables with the gold and crystal that he used only when dining with nobility. He set tables in the dining area, in the courtyards, and by the pools.

Herod had used one of those pools to drown one of the nobles' sons. Jealous Herod was so afraid of this 18-year-old Roman that, in their play and frolic, in the darkness of the evening as others were not watching, Herod had the boy held beneath the water to drown him. That was how evil the heart of this wicked Herod was.

So Herod sent his soldiers to Bethlehem and all through the coasts to invite the new mothers who had recently brought forth to honor them in the presence of Herod the king, to sit among the nobles and drink of the king's wine. Herod brought them to the palace in the king's chariots. The Roman soldiers took the chariots that belonged to the army to take the mothers to the palace. They told the mothers, "You do not need a denarius in order for me to honor you. You do not need a coin or a ticket. You must bring your newborn son. The mothers of the sons of Bethlehem have an invitation to the feast." That was all it took for the egos of those mothers to bring their baby sons to the feast.

The servants told each mother at the door, "We will take your son and care for him. You may be free to feast and dine." Those gullible Judean mothers left their babies in the hands of the soldiers at the door and lined the banquet halls. Soldiers took the babies to the balconies 40 feet above the courtyard and flung them to the ground below. While the mothers of Judah were eating, dining and dancing in this mock celebration, the soldiers went down the cobblestones to any child that still moved. "Any child that yet moveth," in the words of Josephus, they took by the heels and swung its head against the wall. So bitter was Herod's heart against that one Messiah that he killed every son of Bethlehem.

Messiah has come. Shall we weep? The weeping that followed this terrible event was so prominent and so awesome that it even found its way into the Bible. Josephus said that the mothers did not ride the chariots home. Drunken mothers sorted through the piles of small flesh for one glimpse of their babies. They draped the broken bodies of their sons in their arms and walked and walked and wept. As these mothers carried their broken dead children back to Bethlehem, the mourning over their sons and the weeping of their soul was so hideous that Josephus said they could hear Jeremiah from his grave.

> *Thus saith the Lord; A voice was heard in Ramah, lamentation, and bitter weeping; Rahel* [Rachel] *weeping for her children refused to be comforted for her children, because they were not.*
>
> Jeremiah 31:15

Jeremiah had prophesied it.

Herod tried again to bring banquets and do great things for these people. But they refused from then and forever to have anything to do with this hideous man. They could not be comforted. He could not take away the promise.

Overcoming the Herod of Flesh

Any time Messiah, the promise of revival, comes to a city or a church, if there is a Herod on the throne, the flesh will do everything in its power to destroy its possibility.

I have watched the struggle in the church world between the flesh and the Spirit for many years. However, the glory of the Lord is always watered with the tears of hope and patience. There must be a weeping and a supplication for the things of God. If the anointing is not on the throne, Herod will be on the throne.

Herod is jealous. Herod is jealous of the song leader and of the pastor. Herod is bitter. He is bitter at all saints. He is bitter at all Scripture and at all possibility.

> *For His anger endureth but a moment; in His favour is life: weeping may endure for a night, but joy cometh in the morning.*

> Psalm 30:5

The weeping of the sanctuary should be the weeping for a season. Supplication arrests the hopeless weeping of the saint. Joyful revelation replaces that weeping in the dawning of His morning. We do not sorrow forever, but there must be tears. Unfortunately, the tears that are wept in most congregations are tears of lost years, bitter anxiety, enslavement and chains, jealousy, wishes for pre-eminence. The Church could exchange those tears for precious supplication.

In this haunting last day, the shadows of cities and towering buildings fall across rivers, lands and bays. The open countryside is filled with languishing farmers without rain. This country's cold is colder and its heat hotter than it has ever been. In spite of our prayers, there is crime, murders and all manner of nasty things still unleashed and running wild. The Church of the living God is the only answer for this age and the only salvation for this day. If we shut our mouth, evil reigns. If we anoint ourselves with the tears of supplication, the glory of God will climb on our throne.

It is possible for us to put such an anointing on the throne of each one of our hearts through prayer and seeking after God that we may prevail like Hannah when she laid her face against the temple pillar and wept. That type of weeping was rewarded in a handful of months by a precious man child, eight pounds of love in her arms against her bosom. The Church may weep in supplication and find reward in anointing. However, if the Church allows the flesh to be on the throne, it will suffer forever the lamentation that no one can comfort. Jeremiah will cry from his grave.

The Prayer of Supplication

Hannah's weeping was a prayer of supplication that brought something Herod always seeks to destroy. Hannah's weeping brings direction from God. What Hannah was praying for was a boy. She told God, "If You will give me a son, I will lend him to You all his life.[6] She did not say she would give him; she said that she would lend him.

Hannah kept the mortgage and title of Samuel's heart so she could pray for him again in life as she prayed for him in the deadness of her womb. Hannah's prayers could sustain the little boy she had left with only a coat. It must have been a rending time for her to take his little hand and push him toward the old priest Eli whose own sons were full of Belial (Hophni and Phinehas were full of iniquity), watch him disappear between the flickering candles of the temple, and know that she had physically lost him forever.

Likewise, we do not see the Christ we love. The only reason we have not seen Him is because we cannot catch His sight. But we can be closely associated with Him in prayer between the flickering candles of this passing age. The essence of His presence in anointing can always be here.

The candle was dim in the temple when Samuel was a boy. That mean that the direction of the church was fading quickly. The Church must have direction. Hannah wanted a boy, but her supplication gave her more. God has a way of taking the amount of vision a person dares to dream of and magnifying it. God gave something back to Hannah. God took it and rubbed His hand across the ceiling of the temple. Before the candle went out, God said, "Samuel! Samuel!" Samuel answered, "I am here. Your servant hears."[7] God used Samuel, Hannah's vision, to give Israel direction. The Church needs the voice of God and direction. If the Church ever gets a Samuel, the Church can speak to the ghetto. The Church can speak to the rotting flesh of this generation and see them healed.

Consider David as he wept in the cave at Engedi. Consider him as he bowed his head over the robe of the man he honored as the anointed king, Saul. Saul walked right back out of the cave.[8] Many would feel that God had given provision for reason. It was only reasonable that David, who already had the sticky oil of the anointing in the locks of his head from the horn of Samuel, would destroy his enemy in a moment in a cave. However, God gave a higher calling to this man, David, by backing him out of those circumstances.

That did not happen because David was smart. David was only a poor shepherd boy whom God called from following the ewes heavy with lamb. He was just a little ruddy-faced, red-headed kid called up by his brothers in anxiety when they were not chosen king. He was the last one considered.[9] Yet his weeping and his lending and his submission to the anointing was so gloriously taken by his God that the Lord turned his anxiety of 15 years, from the oil to the gold and from the anointing to the crown, into a praise that becomes our song today.

Keeping God in Our Heart

If Herod ever gets the throne of direction in a church, that church is a wandering fool. If Herod can get on the throne, the praise of that church will die. Do you know what will conquer instead? Reason will conquer. We will reasonably kill our enemies. We will reasonably fail to deal with the poor. We will reasonably not give up what we should. We will reason our way into becoming the contentious congregation that so many denominations already are. If we could keep the praise of God tearfully in our hearts, then we might say, "Out of the depths have I cried unto Thee, O Lord."[10] We will sing a glorious song of opening the everlasting gates, and of letting the King of glory come in.[11]

> *By the rivers of Babylon, there we sat down, yea, we wept, when we remembered Zion. We hanged our harps upon the willows in the midst thereof.*
>
> Psalm 137:1-2

The people in bondage wept. They hung their harps on willows. God's dealings with the people of Israel and their weeping teaches us that, as long as Herod is king, bondage will always be the comeback of the Church. It's a cycle—once set free, again in slavery.

> *But now, after that ye have known God, or rather are known of God, how turn ye again to the weak and beggarly elements, whereunto ye desire again to be in bondage?*
>
> Galatians 4:9

How can you turn again to the beggarly elements of the world after the Spirit has liberated you? How do you think you can now live for God in the flesh?

As our ensample, Israel teaches us through its captivity that weeping and supplication should be for a continual renewing of the Holy Ghost. We cannot give up simply because we have a setback. We cannot surrender because we have been taken captive. We must not lose God. Days of prayerful, tearful consecrated prayer so mellows the spirit of man that he needs no other succor, no other helper, no earthly substance other than the glory of God in His temple.

The people of Israel showed by their weeping that they would not endure enslavement. They continually sought liberation. That is the attitude the Church must have today.

Other Kinds of Sorrow

The response to Israel's weeping came in the form of Nehemiah, who stood before the king with his face fallen. Nehemiah said, "I am not just sad. This weeping is not the sadness of the world."[12]

There is another kind of sorrow—the sorrow of those in the world, those who do not have hope.

But I would not have you to be ignorant, brethren, concerning them which are asleep, that ye sorrow not, even as others which have no hope.

I Thessalonians 4:13

There is the lonely desperation of people who gather in a sanctuary, knowing that there is no other help and no other hope. There is no other God. Bricks and mortar are not substantial fortresses. Fires do not always warm. The street is not a friend. The only substantial place of safety is in the glory and the presence of the Lord God.

I have preached in hundreds of those places where there was nothing but the formal captivation of the gothic procedure. Everybody went through their ritual and when they were through, they had been to church.

I stood on the marble floors of St. Patrick's Cathedral and watched them come by the thousands to the mass. I walked around and looked up the center chancel until I could see the man in white speaking out the mass. I watched the people with their heads bowed, flocking in and standing by the thousands on the outside to get back in. Those people feel that just a handful of minutes in a building with some words being spoken will absolve them. Such a dead and cold religion is that. Many of those people were sincerely hungry and thirsty. I wanted to preach or cry aloud. I wanted to say something in that house. I cannot stand the loneliness of procedural bondage.

Thank God for the Holy Ghost who saves us and makes us shout. Thank God for tambourines and bongo drums. Let's not ever let Herod get the throne.

Let the priests, the ministers of the Lord, weep between the porch and the altar....

Joel 2:17

There was also a lamentation and a story among the prophets in Ezekiel's day that said that the time of the prophecy had ceased. It was a proverb that the vision had ceased and there would be a prolonging. "Someday, sometime, somewhere, God will do something."

And the word of the Lord came unto me, saying, Son of man, what is that proverb that ye have in the land of Israel, saying, The days are prolonged, and every vision faileth? Tell them therefore, Thus saith the Lord God; I will make this proverb to cease, and they shall no more use it as a proverb in Israel; but say unto them, The days are at hand, and the effect of every vision.

Ezekiel 12:21-23

The Lord came blazing back through the prophet and said, "I will strip away from Israel the proverb that says, 'The time of the vision is prolonged.' I am taking that away from the Church. That is Herod's tomb." That sounds like Jeremiah out of his grave. Everything the prophets ever said will be fulfilled in Christ. So we need a different crying song. We need to weep between the porch and the altar.

And it shall come to pass afterward, that I will pour out My spirit upon all flesh.

Joel 2:28a

And the sons of strangers shall build up thy walls, and their kings shall minister unto thee: for in My wrath I smote thee, but in My favour have I had mercy on thee. Therefore thy gates shall be open continually: they shall not be shut day nor night; that men may bring unto thee the forces of the Gentiles, and that their kings may be brought. For the nation and kingdom that will not serve thee shall perish; yea, those nations shall be utterly wasted.

Isaiah 60:10-12

And in the days of these kings shall the God of heaven set up a kingdom, which shall never be destroyed: and the kingdom shall not be left to other people, but it shall

> **break in pieces and consume all these kingdoms, and it shall stand for ever.**
>
> Daniel 2:44

The Bible teaches us in the Books of Isaiah and Daniel that He will give the kingdoms of the world to the saints.

There are other prophetic theologies in which we can get caught up. I understand about Armageddon. I know all about the falling away. I know all about being caught away and coming back again, and the marriage supper of the Lamb. All those things concern us in such collateral detail that, when we get through talking about them, we are not sure whether we are staying for the tribulation or leaving in the rapture.

I have come to believe that God does not want His Church so longing and set on prophetic ideas that they cannot live in the present in the power of God. We need to say, "God will do everything He said He would do in His Church," instead of saying, "Someday, somewhere, sometime." Let the weeping spirit of the prophet Joel fall on the Church so much that we will start saying, "God, do not prolong this vision anymore." Today is the day God wants to do the greatest work He has ever done in the world.

Messiah has come. Shall we weep? Yes, we shall. We rejoice in His glory and in His praise. If we rejoice in Messiah, our weeping is but for the night. If Herod remains, our lamentation is forever. The cities will never hear.

When Jesus stood by the grave of Lazarus, He wept for their unbelief. He wept, and then raised the dead.[13]

Some of us cannot minister without the burden and love of this weeping supplication. The worldwide vision will be in the major cities of the world. The powerful ministry of supplication and intercession will accomplish the worldwide vision. It will not be by might nor by power, but by the Spirit of the living God.[14] Our weeping should not be sorrow for loss. Our weeping should be but for a moment, and then we watch Him raise the dead. The Messiah has come. Shall we weep?

End Notes

1. Luke 2:16.
2. Matthew 2:8.
3. Isaiah 35:6.
4. Luke 2:1-3.
5. John 4:25.
6. I Samuel 1:26-28.
7. I Samuel 3:10.
8. I Samuel 24.
9. I Samuel 16:6-12.
10. Psalm 130:1.
11. Psalm 24:9.
12. Nehemiah 2:1-3.
13. John 11:35; 43-44.
14. Zechariah 4:6.

Chapter 9

Conquering the Slave Mentality

He shall judge Thy people with righteousness, and Thy poor with judgment. The mountains shall bring peace to the people, and the little hills, by righteousness. He shall judge the poor of the people, he shall save the children of the needy, and shall break in pieces the oppressor. They shall fear Thee as long as the sun and moon endure, throughout all generations. He shall come down like rain upon the mown grass: as showers that water the earth.

Psalm 72:2-6

Be astonished, O ye heavens, at this, and be horribly afraid, be ye very desolate, saith the Lord. For My people have committed two evils; they have forsaken Me the fountain of living waters, and hewed them out cisterns, broken cisterns, that can hold no water. Is Israel a servant? is he a homeborn slave? why is he spoiled?

Jeremiah 2:12-14

The word *spoiled* here means "taken away." Someone comes in and robs you, or pillages and tears your house apart. "Spoil," in this instance, does not mean spoiling a child. It means, "Why is he torn up and taken away and in bondage?"

Going On to Revival

The gathering back and the revitalizing of that which is spent, spoiled or deteriorated concerns me. Walking with God, finding the Lord in regeneration, and changing into new creatures is not the whole of Kingdom living.

The Word of God teaches us that we cannot exist on a one-time experience with God. Unfortunately, it is the habit of people who have known great experiences in God to rest on those laurels and to dust off their trophies of past conquests. We have a habit, when asked about our relationship with God, of citing some past spiritual thing, and saying, "The Lord saved me 31 years ago." If we manage to escape the trap of depending on past experience, then a helpless and faithless future confronts us. We say, "We will have a revival." When asked, "When will we have a revival?" we have no answer because we did not lay the foundation for spiritual revival. We are not willing to endure the reckless abandon that the heart must have to produce a great spiritual awakening. Instead we shake, wail and hide from the possibility of being removed from our comfortable Christianity.

Future revival is never revival. Yesterday's revival is never revival. The only time there is in God is now. When yesterday was here, it was now. Tomorrow will be now when it arrives. If we have no revival in the now, we will never have it. If we never have a revival, we will die the death of the slothful. We will succumb to the wiles of comfortable Christian living. Therefore we must make up our mind that whatever it costs, we personally will pay that price to obtain what we must have and to become what we must be in Christ Jesus.

Revival costs something. Revival always did cost something. The great awakening of the early church cost those believers imprisonment and the deprivation of earthly comforts. They took all their belongings, laid them at the preacher's feet, and said that nothing they had in this world was their own.[1] They became pronounced paupers in quest of that great tide of revival.

By his own testimony, the apostle Paul was shipwrecked, beaten, stoned and left for dead with almost 300 stripes across his bent back.[2] The Scriptures hint that he was physically impaired and almost blind. Whether you accept his thorn in the flesh as being physical or as a buffeter in the spirit, he was a tormented, chastised human who said, "I have fought a good fight...I have kept the faith."[3] He was not a conveniently comforted soul. He was a hurting, bleeding, lumpy piece of mortality.

If we plan to have twentieth-century revival, we should look in our spiritual checkbook to find out how much is in our account. Revival will cost every dime of that, plus whatever resource our prayerful soul can muster.

Those who are into this business for the cheery ride, the high tone of the choir, or the salving speech of the preacher, will not be very happy with the price of revival. Truth in its naked revelation shows us that many who claim liberty and freedom in this Pentecostal experience and who hope in regeneration are homeborn slaves to a religious bondage that is rampant in our spiritual society today.

The Heavens Have Blushed

Jeremiah was so moved by his heavenly revelation of earthly problems that he said even heaven would blush and fear. When Jeremiah said, "Be astonished, O ye heavens," he was not talking about only the firmament that is above the firmament. Very often, as in this passage prophetically, the heavens speak of all that the heavens hold. Stars and space are certainly included. Would that also include the unseen, innumerable heavenly hosts who are somewhere scattered throughout the ethereal realm, waiting for one command from God to move for God's redemption and for His people? What about the ten thousand times ten thousand, and thousands of thousands of angels, including the cherubim, all the spiritual forces in the angelic realm, who watch the Father's face with intense anticipation, willing to move at a moment's notice in spiritual ministry? How about the heavens filled with angelic force? Does it include the firmament in their flickering, glistening glow? What about the sun and the moon?

Jeremiah said everything needs to blush. The stars need to pull the switch and turn off their lights. The moon needs to blush its face with dust, and the sun needs to cover its face with sackcloth. There is nothing in the heavens that should not be moved by those earthly problems. If they astonish the heavens, how should the earth react? If it moves deity with embarrassment, how should mortals respond?

Be astonished, O ye heavens, at this, and be horribly afraid....

Jeremiah 2:12

Anything that makes heaven scared should scare us to death. What is it that should scare us so? Is it a scaly, fire-breathing monster with three toes that stepped down the Milky Way? Is it an awful beast that plunged its head out of the fiery torment of eternity? The thing that astonished this prophet and all of heaven is simply that the people of God had forsaken the fountain of living water.

Return to the Fountain

How can the Church, the people of God, fall chained at the feet of satanic forces when they are the children of God? Why do God's people drink out of dusty, dingy cisterns when they have a flowing fountain of living water available to them? Why would you have religion when you can have Jesus? Why would you have a creed when you can have the Word of God? Why do you live in a textbook when you can know the living revelation of His power and of His Word?

We still live in the revelation of His power and His Word. Not long after Pentecost and its rushing glorious indwelling and infilling, John took up his pen to write. Now, John had been there. He had seen the first glorious spurts of that rushing artesian well. John had been there when it gushed out and siphoned over the threshold and down the stairs of that old temple upper room into the narrow streets of Jerusalem. John did not just get some phantom revelation at Patmos. He had been there in the first blaze initiation of the Church. He had seen it in its glory. He had seen it in its baptism. John knew it in its power and in its fire.

Later in his life John was an outcast in society. In his prophetic writing, as he stood above the ocean's throbbing monotony and the crying of the vulturous gulls, he wrote about the churches. Just a handful of years past the inception and birth of these churches, he wrote about them, saying, "I have somewhat against thee."[4]

There should have been a spread of a few hundred years before the Church needed to repent. Instead the Church was

just spitting distance from the upper room and already needed to repent. He wrote, "Repent and do your first works over
again, or else."[5] That is a strong message. It sounds like a
threat. You could take someone to court for language like
that. When you say, "or else," you lay down a mandate. You
put down a gauntlet. You are saying, "You do it or something
will happen." That is what God said to His churches in this
part of the Book of Revelation. "Either return to your first
desire, that first love, that first throbbing, glorious impetus
that drove you into the streets and filled Jerusalem with your
doctrine, or I will take your candlestick away. You will no longer be a church."[6]

Why was such a rebuke necessary? Why did the Church
need repentance so soon? We can find the answer in the
mentality of slavery.

The Slave Mentality

The story of slavery in this country is one of the saddest
of all the tales told in American history. It is sad that this nation should have involved itself in the trading of human life.
What tragedy for all men! What tragedy in the throbbing drums
of Pickett's march, in the blazing, fiery muzzles of those can-
nons filled with chain and grapeshot, and in the terrible ex-
plosions and amputations. They waded knee deep in human
blood to pick up 14,000 dead in fewer than 60 minutes at
Gettysburg. You cannot help but hurt when you go back
through pages of history or walk over grassy mounds where
they backed their cannon fire.

Martin Luther King, Jr., cried in Washington's streets above
the heads of masses of those who were the children of the
children of slaves. He cried, in effect, "Thank God Almighty,

we are free again. I have a dream, that all men will someday be free." How many men died with chains around their necks and arms and ankles? How many died beaten to death at whipping posts because they did not nod in time or move quickly enough?

If there is anything more tragic than someone being enslaved, it would have to be someone who is born a slave, a homeborn slave. There is something different in the spirit of a man who has been overcome. If a man has been free and then becomes a slave, he compares his slavery with his past liberty. That is why the Israelites hung their harps on willow trees and refused to sing. "How shall we sing the Lord's song in a strange land?"[7]

A homeborn slave, however, does not consider his slavery strange. Slavery is natural to him. Slavery is his home. To those Jews whom Nebuchadnezzar carried away, Babylon was not home. Babylon was not home to Daniel, to Shadrach or to Meshach. Abednego hated Babylon. The Chaldean language was a strange chirping noise in the ears of these Israelites. They were born free men and were made slaves. They could compare their slavery with even one day's liberty. They could compare walls with open fields. They knew how to compare the song of a bird and play it on a lute. They understood how to pull music out of the air. They could pull a melody they knew from the stream because they had spent hours and days as free men.

A man who is born a slave does not know how to compare his life as a slave with a life of liberty. He just accepts his slavery. That is why some of the black people in our society seem to be almost impossible to educate. Do not blame that problem on a whole race of people, though. The color of a man's skin does not make him able or unable to learn. God makes no difference between skin colors. Only the color of sin matters to God.

If a black man is taught, he may become a statesman. If you put the Word of God in a black preacher, you cannot equal his ability to draw on present truth and circumstance.

What hinders the black man? What hinders the Chinese? It is not the color of their skin. If a man has a slave's mentality, then he will grow up needing someone to tell him what to do, whether he is white or black. If a man has a ghetto mentality, he will expect to get his food and sustenance by some rebellious activity, no matter what color his skin is.

If he is a homeborn slave, he will not have that keen cutting edge of ambition, for desire is made possible by the power of comparison. That is why the man tries to break free of his cell. That is why he will spend years devising some plan that will be fulfilled in minutes to get him out and away from his prison.

People in concentration camps in a time of war spend their living hours without hope and feeling for life, regardless of the abuse they receive at the hands of other men, because they remember their loved ones and because they know the thrill of freedom. They endure unbelievable chastisement and ungodly physical abuse and misuse of their bodies. They endure it when they could die because they have a means of comparison. They remember what it is like to be free. They were not homeborn slaves. They had the cutting edge. The desire is still there, a hunger to escape and a thirsting for liberty. The power of comparison gives men that.

When you live in a church or stay in a spiritual state long enough to forget the sweet breeze of God and the sweet glory that sweeps across your soul in a moment's repentance, when you forget how good it feels to be freed of lust, dirt and filth in your heart, then you become the child of bondage. You are no better than a homeborn slave. There is no cutting edge in your spirit. Do not let your church ever live long enough to breed and birth slavery, for that slavery is the worst kind.

You may be filthy in your sin and you may be foul in your corrupt spirit, but if you can remember the sweet zephyr of the glory of God and entertain the preciousness of His mercy and forgiveness in your heart, then you have a fighting chance of being renewed in the Holy Ghost.

On the other hand, if you lose your sense of comparison and become too dull to remember what it means to run through an open field, climb a tree, or swim through a river, a whip will make you happy. It makes you glad to have a preacher tell you what to do. You will not feel like praying unless someone makes you do it. You need somebody to push you all the time. You might be called a lazy, no-good soul. You are, in actuality, a homeborn slave—born that way, raised that way, happy that way. You do not want to be free.

Many slaves at the time of the Emancipation Proclamation did not want to leave their masters and be free. The proclamation was made that all men were to be free. There were no more slaves in these United States. There were no bought or sold men. Everyone was free. Unbelievably, there were men and women who fearfully, in spite of the physical abuse they had borne through the years, fell down at the feet of their masters and pleaded not to be sent away. "We would not know how to live, master. You took care of us all our lives, master. Do no send us away."

What were they saying? They were homeborn slaves. They did not know to live like free men. Our society still suffers from that heritage. Many black people still suffer because nobody has told them that they are as good as everyone else. If no one does that, they do not have a chance or an opportunity, no matter what society gives them.

We offer them opportunity on one hand, and on the other abuse them mentally, by still considering them as being lesser. They need to understand that they are God's children. They are as good as every other man who was born, breathes air and has red blood flowing through his veins. When people are made to understand that, they talk and act differently. They are invigorated, full of vitality, and motivated.

Why does the Church go on for years and never have revival? Why are we willing to live in yesterday's victory? We have very little sense of comparison left. If the Church does not have revival soon, our children and our children's children will not even remember what it was to be free.

Is Israel a servant? Is the Church a homeborn slave? That mentality must leave the Church. That attitude must leave the mind of the saints of God.

Spiritual Bondage

In this mentality, we are afraid to encounter tribulation. Trials shake us up. We hate suffering. We do not want anything uncomfortable to happen to us. Without knowing it, we are in bondage to an attitude of "Leave me alone."

We have a certain mindset about "bondage." When we say, "This church is in bondage," everybody starts thinking about what people wear because that has been such a taboo in our minds not only in our past, but also in our present.

There is such a lust in the heart of people to be like others that many search for a license for worldliness. We will hold on to a banner of liberty if it will give us an excuse to do anything that we want. That way we can justify our actions. Does righteousness become righteousness because somebody pronounces it to be so? Are we righteous because we meet the code decided by a board, union or churchy group of pastors? Do we please God because we please men?

Where is that keen, cutting sense of right doing that should be the reaction and the direct result of regeneration in the heart? A person who has God in his life should be different.

> *Therefore if any man be in Christ, he is a new creature: old things are passed away; behold, all things are become new.*

II Corinthians 5:17

Why do we look for a place to store old things if they are passed away? We are homeborn slaves. It satisfies us to have the old things as long as we can license them. It satisfies us to have the old lusts as long as we can call them something else. It satisfies us to watch filthy things, to have filthy things around us, or to communicate filthy things, as long as we can justify them religiously.

Truth, on the other hand, is free. Truth does not hide behind clothing. Truth has no facade. Truth is God. Whatever He is, He is. You do not have to say what He is; He is what He is. God did not say, "I am what you want Me to be." He said, "I am that I am."[8] Whatever God says He is, is what He is, not what you say He is.

If God says He is a healer, then every other creed in the world is wrong because God is a healer. He said He was. Let God be true. If He said He would heal your body and take away that sickness, He will not lie to you. He will tell you the truth.

> ***And said, If thou wilt diligently hearken to the voice of the Lord thy God, and wilt do that which is right in His sight...I will put none of these diseases upon thee...for I am the Lord that healeth thee.***

Exodus 15:26

The Lord is not talking to a specific generation or to a group of people on the other side of this continent. He is talking to men who are freeborn men. If you have a slave mentality, you will never be healed. But if you rise and say, "God is my Father and if He said it, it must be true. He would not lie to me." The prison house will then break down. You would be set free.

We have truth in tribulation. That seems to be a paradox, especially to homeborn slaves, because they want people to do things for them. Homeborn slaves consider these trials and tribulations simply as a part of life. Thus they put their heads down and struggle along. That mentality erases the spiritual meaning of the trial and steals the prize that they could win by enduring. A homeborn slave mentality steals the victory that we would have if we kept our conversation clean and in faith.

A Need for Trials

When David prayed a prayer for his cleansing, he did not ask for the eradication of spiritual problems. He said, "Search me and know my heart." After he finished that, he said, "I want God to try me."[9] Have you ever prayed for trials? Why would David pray for a trial? Why would he be ignorant enough to pray for a trial?

154

It is in that sense of tribulation that you find comparison. Without tribulation, you do not know when you are free and when you are bound. The Christian church has put tribulation, trials and problems away as just being a part of life. Believers have forgotten that there is a spiritual happening in every tribulation. That fiery trial works something in you. Tribulation works patience, which in turn also has a work. So the trial of your faith is precious. Don't think it strange when you fall into various temptations. We cannot afford to misunderstand an unbelievable, unanswerable, inexplicable tribulation.

> *And not only so, but we glory in tribulations also: knowing that tribulation worketh patience; and patience, experience; and experience, hope.*
>
> Romans 5:3-4

> *Knowing this, that the trying of your faith worketh patience. But let patience have her perfect work, that ye may be perfect and entire, wanting nothing.*
>
> James 1:3-4

> *Beloved, think it not strange concerning the fiery trial which is to try you, as though some strange thing happened unto you.*
>
> I Peter 4:12

When we interpret the trial and tribulation as being something earthy and mundane, something we must learn to live with, we fall into a slave mentality. We no longer have the power of comparison. That power of comparison contains something. When I am in trouble, I know there is a Deliverer. I know it better now than I did yesterday because now I need deliverance. I have a sense of comparison, for I was born free. That is what regeneration did for me. It removed my slave mentality. I stopped saying, "God can" and started saying, "God will." God not only can, but He will.

And, behold, there came a leper and worshipped Him, saying, Lord, if Thou wilt, Thou canst make me clean. And Jesus put forth His hand, and touched him, saying, I will; be thou clean. And immediately his leprosy was cleansed.

Matthew 8:2-3

There was no question in the mind of the leper whether Jesus could. It was just, "Will You do it?" Jesus said, "I will. Go ahead and be whole." Jesus is still saying, "I will." Regeneration gives you the "I will" mentality. The power of comparison cuts a keen line right down the middle of your perception to let you know that you do not like what you are going through. You do not intend to live the rest of your life going through it either. You will not lie down and let it roll back and forth over you, but you will rise up on the Word of God and say, "Jesus, Your freeborn child is here. I am in trouble. It is probably all my doing, but You said You would deliver me in tribulation. You said You would set me free. You said You would be there when I needed You. Come on, Jesus. Answer my prayer."[10]

Search me, O God, and know my heart: try me, and know my thoughts.

Psalm 139:23

David said, "I do not want You to just search me. Try me." What will trying do? It will tell us what is in our thoughts. What will we say when the screws are put on us? "Nobody loves me"? If that is what we say, then that is what has been in our heart. "I do not think that this church has any love." If the screws are put on tight enough, people say a lot of things from their hearts. The trial is there to expose carnality and selfishness. It is only by comparison that we realize that slavery is not for us.

Is Israel a servant? Will the Church merely dry up and blow away? How do we know? We will endure the trial. We want to endure the tribulation. We know by comparison what it means to feel the glory and to have the power and authority and to not live with less than that. Let's have the keen, lean sense of desire for revival. Jesus never said that He would feed the slouchy, mundane and lazy. He said, "They that hunger and thirst after righteousness shall be filled."

Blessed are they which do hunger and thirst after righteousness: for they shall be filled.

Matthew 5:6

Therefore leaving the principles of the doctrine of Christ, let us go on unto perfection; not laying again the foundation of repentance from dead works, and of faith toward God. ... And this will we do, if God permit. For it is impossible for those who were once enlightened, and have tasted of the heavenly gift, and were made partakers of the Holy Ghost, and have tasted the good word of God, and the powers of the world to come, if they shall fall away, to renew them again unto repentance....

Hebrews 6:1,3-6

The people who will have revival are those who, by comparison, know that there is a greater place in God. People who do not know the power of comparison are homeborn slaves. "We have laid the foundation. We have had the regeneration, but we will lay that foundation again...and over and over again." The Church will never have 45 foundations. We must go on to perfection.

End Notes

1. Acts 4:32,34-35.
2. II Corinthians 11:24-25.
3. II Timothy 4:7.
4. Revelation 2:4.
5. Revelation 2:5.
6. Revelation 2:4-5.
7. Psalm 137:2-4.
8. Exodus 3:14.
9. Psalm 139:23.
10. Psalm 91:15.

Chapter 10

Breaking the Yoke

Cry aloud, spare not, lift up thy voice like a trumpet, and shew My people their transgression, and the house of Jacob their sins. Yet they seek Me daily, and delight to know My ways, as a nation that did righteousness, and forsook not the ordinance of their God: they ask of Me the ordinances of justice; they take delight in approaching to God.

Isaiah 58:1-2

These people followed every letter of the law to do things correctly. They sought the Lord often, prayed every day and delighted to know God's ways. They loved the Word of God and did righteousness. They did not forsake God and they wanted justice. They also worshiped. We know they worshiped because they took delight in approaching God. They loved God's ordinances; they were willing to do them. They wanted to do the right things for other people.

God's Opinion on Fasting

Wherefore have we fasted, say they, and Thou seest not? wherefore have we afflicted our soul, and Thou takest no knowledge? Behold, in the day of your fast ye find pleasure, and exact all your labours.

Isaiah 58:3

God said that these people fasted and told Him everything they had done for Him. They counted every little thing they had ever done for God and told Him how good they were.

Behold, ye fast for strife and debate, and to smite with the fist of wickedness: ye shall not fast as ye do this day, to make your voice to be heard on high.

Isaiah 58:4

If you fast for strife and debate, do not expect God to hear you in Heaven because that fast does not touch Him.

Is it such a fast that I have chosen? a day for a man to afflict his soul? is it to bow down his head as a bulrush, and to spread sackcloth and ashes under him? wilt thou call this a fast, and an acceptable day to the Lord? Is not this the fast that I have chosen? to loose the bands of wickedness, to undo the heavy burdens, and to let the oppressed go free, and that ye break every yoke? Is it not to deal thy bread to the hungry, and that thou bring the poor that are cast out to thy house? when thou seest the naked, that thou cover him; and that thou hide not thyself from thine own flesh?

Isaiah 58:5-7

It is the Lord's will for us to break these yokes. It is not God's will for us to bow down and moan and groan, to spread sackcloth under us, and to feel sorry for ourselves. It does not matter how much we pray or how much we love the Word of God. How much we want justice, how much we want to do the commandments of God, how obedient we are, or how much we worship does not matter if it all has a basic motivation toward self-interest. God will not give us His greatest blessing if our motivation is not right. For years the motivation in our "spirit-filled churches" has been miserably wrong.

A very selfish feeling hangs around the Pentecostal church. "Give me, give me, give me. O God, help me, help me, help me. Bless me, bless me, bless me." All the time we have the greatest gospel in the world. We have the greatest doctrine because it is the doctrine of the Bible. We do not need to go to a creed book to find out what we believe. We can open the Word of God and find right there, plainly explained, what we believe. However, we generally do not have the excitement, enthusiasm and zeal that the early church had in witnessing of the power and grace of God.

There is a time for everything; there is a time for weeping and a time for rejoicing.[1] Isaiah said, "The fast that I give you is not to bow down your head like a bulrush and to sit on sackcloth and ashes." There is a time for mourning and a time for sorrow of the soul. However, the time you are fasting is not the time for sorrowing and weeping.

The Yoke

What is the yoke that Isaiah speaks of in this passage concerning fasting? A yoke is an instrument of harness. It is normally a wooden collar that binds together the animals that plow. Before the steam engine and the tractor, men used this team of animals. A single mule or horse can plow, but if there's some heavy work, it is normally done by a team. Pulling a wagon is heavier work. An ox can plow, but for a heavy wagon with a heavy load, you want a yoke of oxen. That means two oxen harnessed together by a wooden band, a yoke. A yoke puts two together, to work as a team. Everyone on a team is supposed to work together, just like the eleven on a football team, the nine on the baseball team and the five on the basketball team.

Yokes also tie us up with something. When we say we have a yoke, it is not something that simply hangs around our neck to tie us up and keep us still. When we have a yoke, we are moving. Usually we are going someplace we do not want to go. Someone walks with us, taking us along.

Most of us have a negative idea about yokes. When we have a yoke on us, we also have others beside us, pushing us around, taking us where they want us to go, stopping when we do not want to stop, and going when we do not want to go. Yokes do not consider an individual's will.

> *For the good that I would I do not: but the evil which I would not, that I do. Now if I do that I would not, it is no more I that do it, but sin that dwelleth in me.*
>
> Romans 7:19-20

"The things I would do, I do not. The things I would not do, that I do." Paul is talking about yokes. He is talking about this flesh getting yoked up with things it does not want to do.

The Burden of Yokes

Elisha was plowing with 12 yoke of oxen. He had 24 oxen out there in the field. Each yoke held two oxen. So he was plowing with 12 yoke of oxen when the prophet came and said, "Follow me." Elisha simply threw down the traces, turned around, and walked off behind Elijah. He left valuable farm equipment out there. He did not leave it for long, though. He came back and killed it all. Elisha had a big feast and gave it to his friends. He did not intend to come back.[2]

When we start following God, we need to kill the cows, bake them over the handles of the plow, and keep on walking. Some people, though, always find a little friend and say, "Hey, come over here. I will give you a quarter if you hold these till I get back." Those people then have something to come back to in the world. We, however, need to burn every bridge behind us. We need to break up the plows and the handles, kill the oxen and never return.

Job had five hundred yoke of oxen.[3] That is a thousand oxen. When God gave him back more than he had before, Job had a thousand yoke of oxen.[4] That's a lot of "tractors." It would take a big barn to hold that many tractors.

And they all with one consent began to make excuse. The first said unto him, I have bought a piece of ground, and I must needs go and see it: I pray thee have me excused. And another said, I have bought five yoke of oxen, and I go to prove them: I pray thee have me excused.

Luke 14:18-19

These people in this parable were making excuses for not doing the Kingdom work. The man said, "I bought five yoke of oxen. I cannot go." Most people do not go because they have bought some yokes for themselves. "I cannot make it. I have lots of work to do. I cannot be in church because I have to work. I have a little ringing in my right ear, so I cannot go to church. I have been sniffling. My sinus on my left side has been trickling. I have been hacking and coughing all day and I could not sit through church."

What does sitting have to do with your nose dripping? Just get a big box of tissues and go where you need to go. We have so many yokes hanging on us.

Yokes are also a symbol of national labor. Rehoboam took over his father Solomon's place. The people came to him and said, "King Rehoboam, we have been under a great taskmaster. We have had heavy yokes laid upon us. Your father made our yokes grievous." Rehoboam came back and said, "If you think my dad was tough, my little finger will be thicker than my father's loins. I plan to be meaner than Solomon ever thought to be."[5] The yoke typified labor. The Word of God represents the yoke as a heavy burden to bear.

> *Because thou servedst not the Lord thy God with joyfulness, and with gladness of heart, for the abundance of all things; therefore shalt thou serve thine enemies which the Lord shall send against thee, in hunger, and in thirst, and in nakedness, and in want of all things: and He shall put a yoke of iron upon thy neck, until He have destroyed thee.*

> Deuteronomy 28:47-48

The term *yoke* in its literal sense is something that ties you to something else, to labor with it. It is typical of terrible burdens on both the national and personal level. There are at least three major kinds of yokes.

The Yoke of Responsibility

> *Let as many servants as are under the yoke count their own masters worthy of all honour, that the name of God and His doctrine be not blasphemed.*

> I Timothy 6:1

There is a yoke under which we serve. We should give honor to those who are over us. Men who work for others are under the yoke. Some things we simply cannot avoid. We must go to work. We must do what our supervisors tell us to do. We are all responsible to somebody.

Children need to go to school. They are under the yoke. They need to obtain an education. They think school is a terrible yoke, but there are some things we must do. There are responsibilities in life.

Even if you try to cast away these yokes and rebel against them, you do not escape them. If you do not go to work and do eight hours worth of work for eight hours worth of pay, you do not get a lighter yoke because you cheat. Instead you take on a spiritual yoke. You make your spiritual yoke heavier.

All of us must be faithful under the yoke that is currently in our natural lives. If you push a broom, you should push the best broom in the shop. If you are a tool and die maker, you should calibrate to the finest degree. Your work should not vary. You should not allow anything to slide. Children who love God and who are under the yoke should be very careful not to just get away with whatever they can. All of us need to let God speak to our mind.

Some young men and women who have trouble in school are rebellious against teachers. The Word of God is against them because they are not properly under the human yoke. We have a human responsibility. We cannot afford to let that slide. Those people need to go back and apologize to their teachers. If we humble ourselves under a natural yoke, God will honor us for it and bless us.

The Unequal Yoke

Be ye not unequally yoked together with unbelievers: for what fellowship hath righteousness with unrighteousness? and what communion hath light with darkness?

II Corinthians 6:14

The Word of God has something to say about this second type of yoke, the yoke of man. It says, "Be not unequally yoked together with unbelievers." Young men and ladies should not date outside of a spiritual understanding. If you're a young person, you should not go with an unbeliever. You could bring that person to church, though. You can be a soul winner and bring people to the house of God, but if you get emotionally involved with somebody who does not believe the gospel, you go directly against the Word of God. If you marry an unbeliever, that marriage is like putting your head into an unequal yoke. You put your head in one side of the yoke and the unbeliever puts his (or her) head into the other side. Now you must plow side by side with somebody who does not love God.

Most people commonly understand this Scripture to deal with marriage. However, marriage is not the only thing that yokes us. Business relationships have destroyed and deceived men and women because a business was not spiritually sought or wrought through prayer. There are other circumstances in which saints take their friends and companions from the world also. Unfortunately, some people have lost their souls because they chose their friends from among people who smoked, drank and talked dirty. They found friends who stayed angry and gossiped. It ends up that some people do not like to be around other people in the church because of the things they themselves want to do. So they must find other company to do those things because God's people do not do those things. Thus we can become yoked up, not only in marriage, but also in our relationships with the people we meet day by day.

All our relationships (marriage relationships, working relationships, hobbies, and friendships) must carefully be under a proper yoke.

There is also a yoke in the Kingdom relationship. We have a responsibility to our friends in the Church. Paul called

Epaphroditus a true yokefellow. That passage in the beautiful Book of Philippians calls him a brother, a companion in labor, a fellow soldier, a minister, and a messenger.[6] Paul told him, "I have a little something I want you to do. Do not forget those precious women who labored with us. I know you will not forget them, for you are a true yokefellow. I have enjoyed plowing in the same yoke with you."[7]

There is nothing like getting in a prayer room with somebody, putting your head in the same yoke, and saying, "Let us pull this wagon." There is nothing like being in a service with a true yokefellow, and saying, "Sing that song one more time."

To do that, though, we first need one another to put our shoulders to the wheel in our human relationships. We must be under the yoke in our work. We must be faithful to our supervisors. Second, we must be careful in our relationships not to be unequally yoked together with unbelievers. Third, in our relationships with our brothers and sisters in the Church, we should not throw our head around if we think it would jerk our brother's neck. We should not throw our weight around because a brother or a sister is plowing in the same yoke with us. We have a Kingdom responsibility as the yoke of man.

The Yoke of Christ

Come unto Me, all ye that labour and are heavy laden, and I will give you rest. Take My yoke upon you, and learn of Me; for I am meek and lowly in heart: and ye shall find rest unto your souls. For My yoke is easy, and My burden is light.

Matthew 11:28-30

There is a yoke to Christ. We have the idea that liberty brings no responsibility. The Word of God never teaches that liberty in the faith of Christ removes our responsibility from us. We are co-laborers.

> *For we are labourers together with God: ye are God's husbandry, ye are God's building.*
>
> I Corinthians 3:9

When I take on the responsibility of walking with God, I get in the yoke with Him. The beautiful part about the yoke of God is, He carries the biggest part of the load. Isaiah said, "Surely He hath borne our griefs, and carried our sorrows."[8] When you are in the yoke with Jesus, the burden is not quite as heavy. The tears are not as bitter and the loneliness is not as long. You never have to worry about where the waterhole is. You never need to worry about whether you will get to rest because He makes your yoke easy and your burden light.

When the care is pulling down on our shoulders and we cannot take anymore, we can simply pull back a little and say, "Jesus." He then pulls up beside us and we cast our care on Him because He cares for us.[9] It is great to be in the yoke with Him. He said, "Take My yoke. I will take off the yoke of the devil."[10] The yoke of the devil is a hard and bitter one.

There is always hope in the yoke of God. No man minds laboring if he knows he will go home to a hot meal, a warm shower, a loving kiss, beautiful children, and a home. He does not mind laboring because the responsibility is a light thing.

It was not a heavy thing for Jacob to give seven years to work because he had a beautiful little girl watching him every day as he sorted out the cows and the goats. She followed along and watched him when he led them to the waterhole. Seven years went by just like a day because he had sweet little Rachel watching him. Then he got Leah and had to put in seven more years.[11] For the joy that was set before him, though, he endured the cross.[12]

There is something about plowing with Jesus. He stops at every waterhole. He stops under every shady tree. He has a good shelter every evening. His rest is marvelous. In fact, pulling with Him is the rest. His yoke is so easy that the yoke becomes the rest. The Spirit who subdues you becomes the Spirit who lifts you up. The thing you must obey becomes the thing that gives you courage to walk.

On the other hand, the yoke of the devil becomes heavier and heavier. He does not plow you only during the daytime. He plows you all night long. He does not plow you only through the week. He plows on the weekends too. Neither does he plow only when you are young; you plow in old age also. So his yoke does not get lighter at the end of the day. It gets heavier every year. The habits, addictions and burdens grow heavier. The anxieties, the loneliness and the tears are more bitter. The more you beg for relief and plead for an answer, the more he fills your days with more anguish and makes your nights more unbearable.

The psychiatrist cannot help the burdened with his drugs and medication. Even rich people line up to see their shrinks because they cannot stand that thing in their soul that is so heavy. They cannot live with it. But their habits are so ingrained, they cannot live without them either. They are caught in a yoke that has no hope. There is no heavenly peace. There are no songs of liberty in Zion.

Have you heard the devil write even one song that says anything about a golden, glorious end? His songs always talk about the sensational now. It is the satisfying of self today. It is the lust of the flesh and the scraping of the pus and the manure in a world full of corruption. The devil talks about now, *now*, NOW!

Let's be laborers with God. We do not need the devil's yoke. Himself bore our griefs. Himself carried our sorrows. Let's cast our care on Him, casting our burden upon the Lord. He will take it. He will sustain us.

Joy in Witnessing

So they read in the book in the law of God distinctly, and gave the sense, and caused them to understand the reading. And Nehemiah, which is the Tirshatha, and Ezra the priest the scribe, and the Levites that taught the people, said unto all the people, This day is holy unto the Lord your God; mourn not, nor weep. For all the people wept, when they heard the words of the law.

Nehemiah 8:8-9

Hearing the Word of God and faith in the Word of God should not make us mourn when it comes to the responsibility we have. The responsibility itself can make us mourn, but the Word of God should make us rejoice even if we do not like what it says. It is a light to our pathway and a lamp to our feet.[13] It gives us direction. Even if we do not want to go that way, we still know what the will of God is. We should rejoice in that we are taught, directed and led.

Then he said unto them, Go your way, eat the fat, and drink the sweet, and send portions unto them for whom nothing is prepared: for this day is holy unto our Lord: neither be ye sorry; for the joy of the Lord is your strength.

Nehemiah 8:10

Eating the fat and drinking the sweet is the ministry to the Church. The ministry to the Church blesses us and lifts us up.

Some of the yokes mentioned in Isaiah 58, the passage on fasting, were yokes of strife and debate. They do not refer to strife and debate among ourselves, but to our responsibility to the stranger and the sojourner. We strive and debate with the people to whom we are responsible for reaching. How can we strive or debate with someone we are trying to reach? God said we should not do that. Let's not fast and pray so we can win a doctrinal point with somebody. For years we have built up our doctrinal base until we feel that a person cannot be a soul winner unless he learns enough Scripture to convince people of water baptism, of speaking in tongues being the sign of the witness of the Holy Ghost, and of there being only one God. We attack instantly, without provocation, any idea that does not line up exactly with our own. Even though there are false doctrines completely opposed to the Word of God, they still do not provide us with an excuse for our attitude in coming to the world.

It is a yoke to saddle ourselves with a big responsibility to convert somebody doctrinally. We feel that we have not witnessed to them if we have not converted them in a doctrinal sense. That is not right. There should have been joy in our salvation. That joy should have been our strength. Our doctrine is not our only strength, but our joy is our strength.

...the joy of the Lord is your strength.

Nehemiah 8:10

In Hebrew, this verse does not mean that the joy of the Lord strengthens us, but that the joy of the Lord is our strongest point of offense. The joy of the Lord is the biggest weapon we have in our arsenal. It is the biggest gun we can fire and the biggest bullet we can shoot. The joy of the Lord is our strength.

Our greatest strength is not our doctrinal approach to a sinner. Doctrine is our greatest strength in the Church, but it is not our greatest strength on the offense out in the world. The greatest strength we have on the offense is the joy of the Lord.

Nehemiah said, "Look! You heard the Word of God. You know what we have to do. We cannot oppress the stranger wrongly. We cannot put a man out of our field if he is gleaning. We cannot put away somebody who has a disease because we want them away from our children. We must open our hands to the hungry and to the thirsty. Do not stand around, weeping and mourning, because you found out what we should do. This is a day for rejoicing. Just absorb all you can. Eat the fat, drink the sweet, and send portions to those for whom nothing is prepared. Keep rejoicing because the joy of the Lord is our strength."

The difference in your life is that great, sweet grace of God that you come striding in with. While everybody else is saying, "Oh, no!" you are saying, "It is all right. It will be all right." Where did you get that joy? You did not get it from the world. The world cannot give it. The world cannot take it away. Neither does that joy come because you do not have any trouble.

We tend to always relate our spiritual feelings to our personal involvements. If things are going well for us at home, everything is well at church. If things are fine on the job, then things are fine at home. If things are shaping up financially, then we can give some to the Lord. We relate everything we do to how everything is going with us. The worship of God depends on how we feel. That, however, is not the joy that is our strength.

The joy of the Lord that is our strength is the joy that the world cannot give us. It is the joy that God can give us when the creditors are knocking on the door. It is the joy that God can give us when we do not know if we will be able to make it from week to week. It is the joy God gives us when we do not know where that little girl or runaway boy has gone. It is the joy God gives us when we just hear that our mother has cancer or that our father had a heart attack. It is the joy God gives us to be able to influence somebody else for good even though we do not feel so well.

Joy works in a cycle. You cannot reach anybody if you do not have joy. If you reach somebody, you get joy. The first good shot of joy is when you receive the Holy Ghost. Remember that great joy you received when you first experienced the baptism of the Holy Ghost? In that great, initial thrust of joy, peace and happiness, it did not matter to you if they walked off with your house while you were at that altar. They could have it. Why did that feeling settle down and leave? You did not stop loving God. That lack does not mean you no longer feel God. What was that slap-happy, almost drunk-acting attitude?

> *And be not drunk with wine, wherein is excess; but be filled with the Spirit.*
>
> Ephesians 5:18

The Spirit has a direct connection to a man that is just slap-happy. What is that feeling that sweeps over you when you receive the baptism of the Holy Ghost? Why does that great joy settle down? Its perpetuation is kept only by its use. When you do not use that joy that is in your arsenal as a power to witness to what God has done for you, you lose it. No amount of doctrinal instruction, door-to-door teaching or classroom exercise can give you back enough knowledge, boldness, sales ideas, and success possibilities to match that one feeling you had when you received the baptism of the Holy Ghost. The only way to renew that joy is to renew it in somebody else's life. When it happens to somebody else, you receive that great grace once again. The perpetuation of joy is in giving it!

To Fast and Pray

We fast and pray to break those yokes. We make ourselves feel that God will reward us for the great sacrifice we make and take away the yokes from our lives. However, I do not want to fast merely by bowing down my head like a bulrush or heaping ashes upon myself. I want a fast that will break the yoke.

Why fast and pray? Afflicting one's soul and bowing down the head like a bulrush, sitting in sackcloth and ashes, is not what a fast is about. "I am trying to become humble so I can obtain God." You can never obtain God by being humble. You cannot become humble enough. Instead you become proud of your humility.

Isaiah said this fast is to loose the bands of wickedness and to undo the heavy burden. This fast is to let the oppressed go free and to break every yoke. It is to deal bread to the hungry. Why is it to break yokes?

Let's understand this concept. We are trying to be fruitful, but when we do not have understanding, the seeds are stolen. If somebody does not understand, he may sit on a church bench for the rest of his life, never winning a soul, testifying or witnessing. Why not testify? Why not tell a neighbor? Why not get in the car, go down the road, and knock on the door of the neighbor's house?

Have we realized that we live around people we have never met? Why didn't we meet them? "I do not know. I do not feel like meeting people." That is a heavy yoke. If you were selling vacuum cleaners, you would knock on doors because that puts money in your pocket. The souls of your neighbors are lost; they will spend eternity in hell—and Jesus died for them. What a waste for Calvary, for them not to receive salvation. You are in their neighborhood. You are washed in the blood, even placed there for a reason, as an evangelist to that community, but will you keep your mouth shut simply because it does not put money in your pocket?

If somebody stole your prize dog, you would go from door to door and say, "Have you seen that little white poodle? He is about this long and this high, and he barks at everything. I cannot stand to lose him." You go to the store and put a sign on the window: "Reward."

You have the Holy Ghost, your soul is set free, and you have the greatest grace in the all the world, but you build a thick, high wall around yourself and refuse to tell anybody because you are in bondage. The devil has fooled you into thinking, in your fear of rejection, "They do not want it anyway." Or, "I am too shy." That is a yoke. The devil has you bound with your head down. When will your light break forth? When will you be able to deal your bread to the hungry? All of us need to break every yoke. As long as you plow for the devil, though, you will be too tired to do anything for God.

Instead you want someone to lay their hands on you. You even need something else more than that. You need to recover yourself. Otherwise the devil takes advantage of you every time he gets ready. You need to recover yourself and say, "I do not have to live like this. I will win the lost. I will do whatever I must to break out of this shell I am in."

The Anointing Breaks the Yoke

And it shall come to pass in that day, that his burden shall be taken away from off thy shoulder, and his yoke from off thy neck, and the yoke shall be destroyed because of the anointing.

Isaiah 10:27

Jesus said, in short, "If I by the finger of God cast out Satan, then the Kingdom of Heaven has come nigh unto you."[14] He also said that if we do not obey and walk with God, if we killed those whom God sent among us, and if we did not go into the vineyard and become fruitful, He would take His Kingdom and give it to a nation that would (speaking of the Gentiles).[15] Thus the Kingdom was taken away from the Pharisees and given to the Gentiles. The Kingdom was coming and the Kingdom was going. We want to be in the place where the Kingdom is coming.

The thing that immediately signifies the coming of the Kingdom is the devils being cast out. Immediately! The 70 disciples returned from their little trip and said, "Hey, even the devils are subject to us through Your name. We had a big time casting the devil out."[16] Anytime the Kingdom comes, the devil is cast out.

When the Kingdom comes to a sinner, the devil is cast out. When the Kingdom of God comes to somebody, the devil and his works have to go. The sinner repents of his sin, and sin is cast out. We cannot have both the Kingdom and the sin. We cannot have the Kingdom without repentance. Neither can we have the Kingdom without Jesus and His marvelous name. Any time the Kingdom comes, the name will be there. Also, we cannot have the Kingdom without His Spirit. Then we must become a part of a body. By one Spirit we are all baptized into one body, whether we are Jews or Gentiles, bond or free.[17] We are baptized into the body by that Spirit.

Fruitfulness

There is only one theme in the entire scope of all the parables of the Kingdom of God: fruitfulness! The good seed bears fruit: 30, 60 and 100-fold.[18] The good men are gathered into containers, barrels and vessels. The bad are cast away.[19] The Kingdom is casting out the devil and gathering in the harvest.

At the end of the world, the angels will be the reapers.[20] They will gather the harvest of the Kingdom from every corner of heaven to the corners of the earth.

> *Every branch in Me that beareth not fruit He taketh away: and every branch that beareth fruit, He purgeth it, that it may bring forth more fruit.*

John 15:2

The Church is fruitless because of the work of the devil. Satan is the one who makes us unfruitful. Before he gets his little kingdom re-established in the heart of a believer, that believer may, in his spiritual infancy, be one of the greatest promulgators of the gospel message, even with his limited amount of spiritual understanding. That believer is usually our best candidate as a soul winner because satan was recently cast down in his life. The new believer is not contending with all the little clogged places that the devil continues to put on the saints of God.

> *Ye have not chosen Me, but I have chosen you, and ordained you, that ye should go and bring forth fruit, and that your fruit should remain: that whatsoever ye shall ask of the Father in My name, He may give it you.*
>
> John 15:16

God did not choose you to merely shout and sing, although shouting and singing is a part of the glory of the liberty of salvation. Worshiping God is a part of this great salvation. However, the purpose for your salvation is the very reason you are saved. You have salvation because somebody reached you through prayer or testimony. You are the result of the purpose, which is fruitfulness. The result of the purpose must then become the purpose and so perpetuate itself.

In the beginning of Genesis, fruitfulness was the first command to the man and the woman.

> *And God blessed them, and God said unto them, Be fruitful, and multiply, and replenish the earth, and subdue it: and have dominion...over every living thing that moveth upon the earth.*
>
> Genesis 1:28

The entire story of the Kingdom in the New Testament deals with men not being fruitful because they do not understand the things about the Kingdom.

> *When any one heareth the word of the kingdom, and understandeth it not, then cometh the wicked one, and catcheth away that which was sown in his heart. This is he which received seed by the way side.*
>
> Matthew 13:19

Jesus spoke to the people in parables so they would not understand, but He took the concentrated group of His disciples and poured His understanding into them. He explained to this select group what the parables meant.

"Every branch in Me that beareth not fruit He taketh away."[21] That does not mean He leaves the fruitful branches alone. He cuts them back. Every son He receives, He chastens.[22] There is no such thing as just floating around in the Kingdom of God. You are either being taken away because you are fruitless or the Holy Ghost is working on you so you bear more fruit. There is no neutrality in the Kingdom.

Cleaning the Banks

Once, in a vision, I saw a river. I was standing on a high railing looking down on the river. It was an abundant body of water, but trash was all along the banks. I was telling different people in the church, "You see that paper cup down there? Run down there and pick that up. Get this bank cleaned up. It is messy along the river. We have trash all along the river." There was a bridge across the river and I sent boys to work on the bank on the other side. We soon had the banks so clean, they were sweeping the edge of the river with a broom. It was spick and span. When we finally finished cleaning the banks, I put my hands behind me and looked down, but something was wrong. I heard the voice of the Lord speak to me, saying, "The bank is clean, but the river is still muddy." I asked the Lord, "Why is the river muddy?" The voice spoke to me and said, "Because it is shallow." Anything that moves in it stirs it up.

Then my vision changed, and I was caught up. I thought I was in an airplane because I heard a great roaring. I went out over a great, huge, wide river. It was so wide, I asked the

Lord, "Lord, are the banks clean on this river?" The voice spoke to me and said, "Look and see." But the river was so wide, I could not see either bank. All I could see was the river. It was green, clean and pure.

What does that mean? It means we spend our time cleaning the bank. We clean up the little tricky things that we can see, when we actually need the water to rise. As the water rises, it washes away the debris on the bank. So it is the water we need to get clean. Yet we are busy working on petty things. We are busy picking around at little things in our lives. We need to get down to the heart and soul.

You do not have to beg men and women who love souls to pray and read the Word of God. We have listless Christianity because there is general boredom in the Church. There are no babies in our arms. There are no children at our knees. When new life and fresh blood is absent, all we have to do is sit around and preen one another. We pick out the old feathers from one another. We judge one another.

We clean up the bank of the river, and ask, "Do you like my river?" The river seems fine, but nobody wants to drink water out of that river. Nobody wants to go swimming in that river. Nobody wants to be a part of your church. Why not? After all, the bank is clean. The building is beautiful. The choir sings professionally. The preacher preaches well. It abounds in ushers.

Order is great if it is spiritual, but it is lousy if that's all there is. We need the Spirit of God to rise to an all-time high. We need Him to wash away the trash on our banks. Sin, however, is not the only trash along the banks. Sometimes weights line the banks. We become too busy with carnal things. Somebody told me the one time, "I think I will go to school and take a course. I get tired sitting around the house all day."

It would be great if somebody would take that time and knock on a door, visit a neighbor, read the Word of God, or do something that would benefit the Kingdom. Instead we become tangled up with the cares of life. Now, that is not necessarily sin. But the devil is a master at finding little things that we have to do, and majoring on them. He loves to be able to tell us what to do.

We must lay aside some things in order to be soul winners. Nobody becomes successful unless he replaces something in his life that he considers valuable with something more substantial and productive. Otherwise, we remain the same. We will not have any future productivity unless we exchange our valuables for something else. We cannot live more than 24 hours a day. Actually, we already spend them doing something. So we must replace what we do in that time with something more productive in order to be fruitful. We cannot add six more hours to a day and say, "I will do exactly what I do now, but I will get six more hours to do something else." There must be a replacement of things and time.

Escaping Bondage

Stand fast therefore in the liberty wherewith Christ hath made us free, and be not entangled again with the yoke of bondage.

Galatians 5:1

Wherein I suffer trouble, as an evil doer, even unto bonds; but the word of God is not bound.

II Timothy 2:9

The devil cannot bind the Word of God. When you put on the Word of God, the devil cannot slide a chain on you. That bondage goes straight to the floor. All you need to do is just take one step in the light and you are out of bondage and going on into the productiveness of the Kingdom of God.

The Word of God is one thing the devil cannot stand because there is no bondage in the Word. When you take the Word of God to him, the devil will run every time. When the devil tempted and tormented Jesus, the Lord did not quote axioms or poetic phrases to him. He just said, "It is written."[23] Jesus called on the written Word of God. He did not call up black ink on India paper. He called up spirit and life, the power that has no bondage in it. When He spoke it to the devil, the devil could not stand it.

There are no fences around the Word of God. If you cover yourself with the Word of God, bondage cannot stay. Bondage and chains slide off you. For them, grabbing you is just like grabbing a greased pig. The devil cannot hold on. Every time he thinks he has you, he doesn't, because the Word of God is covering you.

The holy oil of anointing breaks every yoke. The yokes cannot stay on you when you have the oil on you. The Bible says that the anointing would break the yoke.[24] That means all yokes, not just some of them.

What we need, more than anything else, is for God to put our lives in order. We need order in the Church, but we also need our lives put in order: What should I do with my time? How should I bring up my children? What should I do about hobbies, places, things, eating out, and my friends? Can God help us with all that? If we have the anointing on where we go, on what we read, on what we look at, on what we have in our house, and on everything else, there are no yokes. They all slide off because of that anointing.

Unfortunately, we fail to pray about where we go, what we do, and what we say. Instead we do our own thing and live our own lives, only asking God to help us on the side. Once in a while we punch Him and say, "Oh, Jesus, come on in. We have been very busy, but we like You too. We are glad You came to visit." He just visits us.

The people who walk with God, however, are productive. They have Him living in the living room. When they go in the kitchen, He lives in the kitchen. Jesus lives in the bedroom. Jesus lives in the car. Jesus lives on the job. He is a part of them. He walks with them. He talks with them. He is not a visitor. He is more than a casual friend.

Simply Learn

"Take My yoke." What is this heavy yoke of the Lord? It is just learning. When you start learning, the yoke becomes understanding. Then understanding becomes faith. Faith becomes fruitfulness.

And the servant of the Lord must not strive; but be gentle unto all men, apt to teach, patient, in meekness instructing those that oppose themselves; if God peradventure will give them repentance to the acknowledging of the truth; and that they may recover themselves out of the snare of the devil, who are taken captive by him at his will.

II Timothy 2:24-26

Instruction is a key. If we do not obtain understanding, then we will not be fruitful. We cannot cast out the devil if we do not have some understanding. If we do not understand, the devil will take us captive any time he wants. But if we receive understanding, we may recover ourselves. We could wait for the preacher to deliver us, but it would never happen. We can wait for a saint to come by and deliver us, but that will not happen either because these things must come with the renewing of the mind. We must make up our mind that we will not let this spirit do this to us. Someone can pray for us today, and the Lord can deliver us. Tomorrow morning, though, we would be right back in the pigpen where we were.

We need to lay hands on people and cast out the devil, but more than that, we need to teach people to overcome the devil with the Word of God. The saints of God need to know how to oppose and resist the devil.

Until then, anytime the devil gets ready, he just slaps you and you pull right back into his yoke and take off again, plowing for the devil. For a beast to be worked like that, it must be brought under submission. You cannot simply find a horse, mount him, and ride him. Actually, you could get on the horse, but you might not ride him. The horse has to be broken. "His dam and his sire were gentle, so he must be gentle too." No, you must break the colt because the colt will not be gentle. The young ox must be broken. You have to break them, break them, break them, and break them. Then you have to put a bit in the horse's mouth. You must be careful or that animal will kick you, bite you, or step on you. You say, "Oh, he is a gentle thing." About that time, he hits you right behind the head. He can rear up and with one hoof hit you.

A friend of mine, Mr. Darby, was in the hospital almost six months because a big stallion reared up and hit Mr. Darby with his hoof. It pulled the man's face off, nose and everything. The medical team had to pull it all back up and sew it back on.

Was he a good horse? Mr. Darby said he was a good horse. I would have shot that stallion. He said, "I do not want to shoot him. He is a good horse."

That is what the devil does to us. He throws enough weight on you until you break down. Then he'll throw some more weight on you and you break down some more.

We have learned to live without joy. We have settled down to a good doctrinal basis. However, we cannot live on a feeling all the time; our feelings will fool us. We must walk by faith, not by feelings. We walk by faith, not by sight.[25] That pertains to our daily living.

Last Thoughts on Soul Winning

We should not have a haphazard attitude about our responsibility to the world either. When we address somebody negatively and argue a point with them, we usually do not fast and pray for them. What is most infectious in winning souls, however, is the great joy and peace that we have.

There is a doctrine spread all over the church world that says, "People are not hungry for God. They go to other churches because it is easier for them to conform to their doctrines, but they do not want the truth." That is an incorrect yoke that we have hanging around our neck. People are hungry for truth. They will walk into truth if we just lead them instead of beating them to death.

I know preachers who will not baptize a man if his hair is too long. They tell him, "Go get a haircut, boy. Then I will baptize you." Then they will baptize short-haired women. It takes a little longer for hair to grow out than it does to cut it off. They need those converts and those tithes just as soon as they can get it, so they baptize the ladies.

We are hung up on a lot of garbage. How can we expect to win people to God when we approach them so negatively and bring them things that they have not matured enough to understand? We must let the Holy Ghost do the work in those lives.

My father was very patient with people. I would see people come into the church and he would let many things slide. I thought, "He will never tell them what to do. People who visit here will think they are part of us." Then he would rise up and say they were part of us. Those new people were still wearing things we thought they should not wear. They were looking ways, acting ways, and doing things that were not right. I did not know it, but those people were growing. I did not understand that until years later. Then I realized that people, in coming to God, do not suddenly take on every trait of an adult believer. A child at birth does not stand as tall as an adult stands. When you go in to see your baby boy in the nursery of the hospital three days after he is born, you do not walk up and say, "How are you, bud? Good to see you." He has not grown that big that fast. He is still a child. He will act like a child. He will do things that you would not do and act in ways you would not act. Sad to say, believers have never been able to tolerate that in the Pentecostal church.

The people who survive in our churches are the people who conform very quickly to what we believe they should be.

If they conform fast enough, they make it. If they do not conform fast enough, then we somehow manage to destroy them and their faith because of our bowed down, ash heap, bulrush attitude. Debate and strife have no part of soul winning. People are not won to God by fussing.

What is the greatest power we have to win men to God? The joy of the Lord is our greatest strength. "Look what God has done for me. Isn't Jesus wonderful? If you just knew where He brought me from... If you had any idea where I was before He touched me... I found such great happiness and joy." When we can exude that feeling straight from God in the world of crises that we live in, there is no way we cannot be soul winners. It is not, "Please be a soul winner." It is, "How can you help being one?" If we have the Spirit of Isaiah's vision, we do not fast for debate and strife. We do not fast merely to make our voice heard on high, but we fast and pray to feed the hungry, to refresh the thirsty, and to comfort the lonely. "Then shall thy light break forth as the morning, and thine health shall spring forth speedily."[26] The things that have been lonely afflictions in our soul will receive an answer when we let the joy of the Lord pour out of our life.

The apostle Paul and the apostle Peter preached doctrine to the early church. But what would Paul talk about if he was talking to a king or to a governor? He would tell his testimony. "I was on the road to Damascus. A light shone about me and I fell to the earth as dead."[27] He simply would tell his story to a king. What about a text? You do not need a text. Just tell your story. The excitement and joy that came to your life in your transformation is your great strength.

You can lead men to God without knowing one verse from the Bible. If you can lead men to repentance, you can bring them to church with you and disciple them into the fullness of the truth so they may receive salvation. Try to disciple them before you save them. After all, you have to catch a fish before you can scale it. By all means, do not eat them until you scale them. All of us tend, however, to gobble them up before we ever get them on the hook.

If you were very hungry as you were fishing and wanted to eat fish, would you go over to the bank and say, "You better get on my hook. If you do not get on my hook, you will never get on my plate. If you do not get on my plate, you will never be good for dinner. You must understand that you are only a..."

The old fisherman will say, "Shhh. Shut up. Shh! I had better look at my bait again. Hah! I got you." Did you ever know anybody with good sense who went fishing, caught one fish, and said, "I caught a fish. I will see you later"? If you catch one, it just makes you want to catch a whole lot more. Let's go catch a whole batch of fish.

End Notes

1. Ecclesiastes 3:1.
2. I Kings 19:19-21.
3. Job 1:3.
4. Job 42:12.
5. I Kings 12:3-11.
6. Philippians 2:25.
7. Philippians 4:3.
8. Isaiah 53:4a.
9. I Peter 5:7.
10. Matthew 11:28-30.
11. Genesis 29:18-30.
12. See Hebrews 12:2.
13. Psalm 119:105.
14. Matthew 12:28.
15. Matthew 21:43.
16. Luke 10:17.
17. I Corinthians 12:13.
18. Mark 4:20.
19. Matthew 13:48.
20. Matthew 13:39.
21. John 15:2a.
22. Hebrews 12:6.
23. Matthew 4:4,7,10; Luke 4:4,8.
24. Isaiah 10:27.
25. II Corinthians 5:7.

26. Isaiah 58:8a.
27. See Acts 26.

Exciting titles
by Don Nori

THE POWER OF BROKENNESS

Accepting Brokenness is a must for becoming a true vessel of the Lord, and is a stepping-stone to revival in our hearts, our homes, and our churches. Brokenness alone brings us to the wonderful revelation of how deep and great our Lord's mercy really is. Join this companion who leads us through the darkest of nights. Discover the *Power of Brokenness*.

Paperback Book, 168p. ISBN 1-56043-178-4 Retail $9.99

THE ANGEL AND THE JUDGMENT

Few understand the power of our judgments—or the aftermath of the words we speak in thoughtless, emotional pain. In this powerful story about a preacher and an angel, you'll see how the heavens respond and how the earth is changed by the words we utter in secret.

Paperback Book, 192p. ISBN 1-56043-154-7 (6" X 9") Retail $10.99

HIS MANIFEST PRESENCE

This is a passionate look at God's desire for a people with whom He can have intimate fellowship. Not simply a book on worship, it faces our triumphs as well as our sorrows in relation to God's plan for a dwelling place that is splendid in holiness and love.

Paperback Book, 182p. ISBN 0-914903-48-9 Retail $8.99
Also available in Spanish.
Paperback Book, 168p. ISBN 1-56043-079-6 Retail $8.99

SECRETS OF THE MOST HOLY PLACE

Here is a prophetic parable you will read again and again. The winds of God are blowing, drawing you to His Life within the Veil of the Most Holy Place. There you begin to see as you experience a depth of relationship your heart has yearned for. This book is a living, dynamic experience with God!

Paperback Book, 182p. ISBN 1-56043-076-1 Retail $9.99

HOW TO FIND GOD'S LOVE

Here is a heartwarming story about three people who tell their stories of tragedy, fear, and disease, and how God showed them His love in a real way.

Paperback Book, 108p. ISBN 0-914903-28-4 (4" X 7") Retail $5.99
Also available in Spanish.
Paperback Book, 144p. ISBN 1-56043-024-9 (4" X 7") Retail $5.99

Available at your local Christian bookstore.

Internet: http://www.reapernet.com

Prices subject to change without notice.

Other
Destiny Image titles
you will enjoy reading

IT'S THE WALK, NOT THE TALK

by LaFayette Scales.

Lots of people talk about spiritual growth, but how many really demonstrate it? This book outlines and describes six levels of spiritual maturity and shows you how to move up to the higher levels of God's purpose for His children. Start traveling the path to spiritual maturity in Christ because, after all, it's the walk, not the talk, that counts!

Paperback Book, 210p. ISBN 1-56043-170-9 Retail $9.99

WHAT IS THE CHURCH COMING TO?

by LaFayette Scales.

Do you know what the Church is, and what its destiny and purpose are? In *What Is the Church Coming To?* you'll find fresh biblical insight, new studies, and exciting reflections on seven "pictures" of the Church that are found in the Bible. Rediscover today's Church as a powerful, living entity!

Paperback Book, 196p. ISBN 1-56043-169-5 Retail $9.99

THE CLOUD OF GLORY IS MOVING

by Mark Chironna.

One of the most fascinating pictures we have in the Scriptures that describe the appearing of the Lord is the cloud of glory. From the Exodus to the Day of Pentecost to today, the cloud of glory has been moving. This book will help refresh your own passion to move with the cloud. (Previously published as *The Inner Dimension*.)

Paperback Book, 140p. ISBN 1-56043-110-5 Retail $9.99

THE ELISHA PRINCIPLE

by Mark Chironna.

Have you crossed your Jordan? Have you made that step to leave all for the sake of His plan for your life? This book will help you to understand the principles required and make the move you need to make.

Paperback Book, 96p. ISBN 1-56043-006-0 Retail $8.99

Also available in Spanish.

Paperback Book, 96p. ISBN 1-56043-080-X Retail $8.99

THE UNDISCOVERED CHRIST

by Mark Chironna.

There is a desperate need for apostolic and prophetic ministry to preach the message of the Christ and His unfathomable riches in this hour. To fully carry out the mission of Jesus in the earth, we must become intimately acquainted with Him by His Spirit as the resurrected Christ. Within these pages you will find your passion renewed for a fresh revelation of the indwelling Christ!

Paperback Book, 112p. ISBN 1-56043-085-0 Retail $8.99

Available at your local Christian bookstore.

Internet: http://www.reapernet.com

Prices subject to change without notice.